MAKING ALL THINGS NEW

MAKING ALL THINGS NEW

& OTHER CLASSICS ♪ Henri Nouwen

Fount
An Imprint of HarperCollins*Publishers*

Fount is an imprint of
HarperCollins*Religious*
part of HarperCollins*Publishers*
77–85 Fulham Palace Road, London W6 8JB
www.christian-publishing.com

Making All Things New first published in the USA in 1981 by HarperSanFrancisco
Intimacy first published in the USA in 1969 by HarperSanFrancisco
A Letter of Consolation first published in the USA in 1982 by HarperSanFrancisco
The Living Reminder first published in the USA by HarperSanFrancisco

This edition 2000

1 3 5 7 9 10 8 6 4 2

All Bible quotations are from the Jerusalem Bible

A catalogue record for this book is available
from the British Library

ISBN 0 00 628170 2

Printed and bound in Great Britain by
Omnia Books Limited, Glasgow

Contents

MAKING ALL
THINGS NEW

In gratitude for ten joyful years
with students and faculty of the
Yale Divinity School

Contents

Do not worry; do not say, 'What are we to eat? What are we to drink? How are we to be clothed?' ... Your heavenly Father knows you need them all. Set your hearts on his kingdom first ... and all these other things will be given you as well.

Matthew 6:31–33

Acknowledgments

During the past few years, various friends have asked me, 'What do you mean when you speak about the spiritual life?' Every time this question has come up, I have wished I had a small and simple book which could offer the beginning of a response. Although there are many excellent books about the spiritual life, I still felt that there was a place for a text which could be read within a few hours and could not only explain what the spiritual life is but also create a desire to live it. This feeling caused me to write this book. Many of the ideas have been expressed before by others as well as by myself, but I hope and pray that the way they are brought together here will be of help to those who feel 'filled but unfulfilled'.

I want to express my sincere thanks to the Passionist Sisters of Our Lady of Calvary retreat house in Farmington, Connecticut, who by their kindness and hospitality created the quiet space in which this book could be written. I am also grateful for the good advice and enthusiastic support of John Shopp and his colleagues at Harper & Row, and for the generous help of John Mogabgab, Robert Moore and Wil Rikmanspoel in making the manuscript ready for publication. I owe a special word of thanks to the many students of the Yale Divinity School whose insightful criticisms on the first draft made me rewrite many parts of this text. Finally, I want to say thanks to Henry Morris, who suggested the title to me. I hope that all of us who worked together on this book will find that it was a worthwhile ministry.

Introduction

In this book I would like to explore what it means to live a spiritual life and how to live it. In the midst of our restless and hectic lives we sometimes wonder, 'What is our true vocation in life?' 'Where can we find the peace of mind to listen to the calling voice of God?' 'Who can guide us through the inner labyrinth of our thoughts, emotions and feelings?' These and many similar questions express a deep desire to live a spiritual life, but also a great unclarity about its meaning and practice.

I have written this book, first of all, for men and women who experience a persistent urge to enter more deeply into the spiritual life but are confused about the direction in which to go. These are the people who 'know' the story of Christ and have a deep desire to let this knowledge descend from their minds into their hearts. They have a vague sense that such 'heart-knowledge' can not only give them a new sense of who they are, but can even make all things new for them. But these same people often feel a certain hesitation and fear to enter on this uncharted path, and often wonder if they are not fooling themselves. I hope that, for them, this small book offers some encouragement and direction.

But I also want to speak, although indirectly, to the many for whom the Christian story is unfamiliar or strange but who experience a general desire for spiritual freedom. I hope that what is written for Christians is written in such a way that there is enough space for others to discover anchor-points in their own search for a spiritual home. This can only be a true book for Christians when it addresses itself also to those whose many questions about the meaning of life have remained open-minded. The authentic spiritual life finds its basis in the human condition, which all people – whether they are Christians or not – have in common.

As the point of departure, I have chosen Jesus' words 'Do not worry'. Worrying has become such a part and parcel of our daily life that a life without worries seems not only impossible, but even undesirable. We have a suspicion that to be carefree is unrealistic and – worse – dangerous. Our worries motivate us to work hard, to prepare ourselves for the future, and to arm ourselves against impending threats. Yet Jesus says, 'Do not worry; do not say, "What are we to eat? What are we to drink? How are we to be clothed?" ... Your heavenly Father knows you need them all. Set your hearts on his kingdom first ... and all these other things will be given you as well.' With this radical and 'unrealistic' counsel, Jesus points to the possibility of a life without worries, a life in which all things are being made new. Since I hope to describe the spiritual life in which the Spirit of God can recreate us as truly free people, I have called this book *Making All Things New*.

I have divided my reflections into three parts. In the first part, I want to discuss the destructive effects of worrying in our daily lives. In the second part, I plan to show how Jesus responds to our paralyzing worries by offering us a new life, a life in which the Spirit of God can make all things new for us. Finally, in the third part, I want to describe some specific disciplines which can cause our worries slowly to lose their grip on us, and which can thus allow the Spirit of God to do His recreating work.

'All These Other Things'

INTRODUCTION

The spiritual life is not a life before, after, or beyond our every-day existence. No, the spiritual life can only be real when it is lived in the midst of the pains and joys of the here and now. Therefore we need to begin with a careful look at the way we think, speak, feel, and act from hour to hour, day to day, week to week, and year to year, in order to become more fully aware of our hunger for the Spirit. As long as we have only a vague inner feeling of discontent with our present way of living, and only an indefinite desire for 'things spiritual', our lives will continue to stagnate in a generalized melancholy. We often say, 'I am not very happy. I am not content with the way my life is going. I am not really joyful or peaceful, but I just don't know how things can be different, and I guess I have to be realistic and accept my life as it is.' It is this mood of resignation that prevents us from actively searching for the life of the Spirit.

Our first task is to dispel this vague, murky feeling of discontent and to look critically at how we are living our lives. This requires honesty, courage and trust. We must honestly unmask and courageously confront our many self-deceptive games. We must trust that our honesty and courage will lead us not to despair, but to a new heaven and a new earth.

More so than the people of Jesus' day, we of the 'modern age' can be called worrying people. But how does our contemporary worrying actually manifest itself? Having looked critically at my own life and the lives of those around me, two words emerge as descriptive of our situation: filled and unfulfilled.

FILLED

One of the most obvious characteristics of our daily lives is that we are busy. We experience our days as filled with things to do, people to meet, projects to finish, letters to write, calls to make, and appointments to keep. Our lives often seem like overpacked suitcases bursting at the seams. In fact, we are almost always aware of being behind schedule. There is a nagging sense that there are unfinished tasks, unfulfilled promises, unrealized proposals. There is always something else that we should have remembered, done, or said. There are always people we did not speak to, write to, or visit. Thus, although we are very busy, we also have a lingering feeling of never really fulfilling our obligations.

The strange thing, however, is that it is very hard not to be busy. Being busy has become a status symbol. People expect us to be busy and to have many things on our minds. Often our friends say to us, 'I guess you are busy, as usual', and mean it as a compliment. They reaffirm the general assumption that it is good to be busy. In fact, those who do not know what to do in the near future make their friends nervous. Being busy and being important often seem to mean the same thing. Quite a few telephone calls begin with the remark, 'I know you are busy, but do you have a minute?' suggesting that a minute taken from a person whose agenda is filled is worth more than an hour from someone who has little to do.

In our production-oriented society, being busy, having an occupation, has become one of the main ways, if not *the* main way, of identifying ourselves. Without an occupation, not just our economic security but our very identity is endangered. This explains the great fear with which many people face their retirement. After all, who are we when we no longer have an occupation?

More enslaving than our occupations, however, are our preoccupations. To be *pre*-occupied means to fill our time and place long before we are there. This is worrying in the more specific sense of the word. It is a mind filled with 'ifs'. We say to ourselves, 'What if I get the flu? What if I lose my job? What if my child is not home on time? What if there is not enough food tomorrow? What if I am attacked? What if a war starts? What if the world comes to an end? What if ...?' All these 'ifs' fill our minds with anxious thoughts and make us wonder constantly what to do and what to say in case something should happen in the future. Much, if not most, of our suffering is connected with these preoccupations. Possible career changes, possible family conflicts, possible illnesses, possible disasters, and a possible nuclear holocaust make us anxious, fearful, suspicious, greedy, nervous and morose. They prevent us from feeling a real inner freedom. Since we are always preparing for eventualities, we seldom fully trust the moment. It is no exaggeration to say that much human energy is invested in these fearful preoccupations. Our individual as well as communal lives are so deeply moulded by our worries about tomorrow that today hardly can be experienced.

Not only being occupied but also being preoccupied is highly encouraged by our society. The way in which newspapers, radio and TV communicate their news to us creates an atmosphere of constant emergency. The excited voices of reporters, the predilection for gruesome accidents, cruel crimes and perverted behaviour, and the hour-to-hour coverage of human misery at home and abroad slowly engulf us with an all-pervasive sense of impending doom. On top of all this bad news is the avalanche of advertisements. Their unrelenting insistence that we will miss out on something very important if we do not read this book, see this movie, hear this speaker, or buy this new product deepens our restlessness and adds many fabricated preoccupations to the already existing ones. Sometimes it seems as if our society has become dependent on the maintenance of these artificial worries. What would happen if we stopped worrying? If the urge to be entertained so much, to travel so much, to buy so much, and to arm ourselves so much no longer motivated our behaviour, could our society as it is today still function? The tragedy is that we are indeed caught in a web of false expectations and contrived needs. Our occupations and preoccupations fill our external and internal lives to the brim. They prevent the Spirit of God from breathing freely in us and thus renewing our lives.

UNFULFILLED

Beneath our worrying lives, however, something else is going on. While our minds and hearts are filled with many things, and we wonder how we can live up to the expectations imposed upon us by ourselves and others, we have a deep sense of unfulfilment. While busy with and worried about many things, we seldom feel truly satisfied, at peace, or at home. A gnawing sense of being unfulfilled underlies our filled lives. Reflecting a little more on this experience of unfulfilment, I can discern different sentiments. The most significant are boredom, resentment and depression.

Boredom is a sentiment of disconnectedness. While we are busy with many things, we wonder if what we do makes any real difference. Life presents itself as a random and unconnected series of activities and events over which we have little or no control. To be bored, therefore, does not mean that we have nothing to do, but that we question the value of the things we are so busy doing. The great paradox of our time is that many of us are busy and bored at the same time. While running from one event to the next, we wonder in our innermost selves if anything is really happening. While we can hardly keep up with our many tasks and obligations, we are not so sure that it would make any difference if we did nothing at all. While people keep pushing us in all directions, we doubt if anyone really cares. In short, while our lives are full, we feel unfulfilled.

Boredom is often closely linked to resentment. When we are busy, yet wondering if our busyness means anything to anyone, we easily feel used, manipulated, and exploited. We begin to see ourselves as victims pushed around and made to do all sorts of things by people who do not really take us seriously as human beings. Then an inner anger starts to develop, an anger which in time settles into our hearts as an always fretting companion. Our hot anger gradually becomes cold anger. This 'frozen anger' is the resentment which has such a poisoning effect on our society.

The most debilitating expression of our unfulfilment, however, is depression. When we begin to feel not only that our presence makes little difference but also that our absence might be preferred, we can easily be engulfed by an overwhelming sense of guilt. This guilt is not connected with any particular action, but with life itself. We feel guilty being alive. The realization that the world might be better off without the soft drink, the deodorant, or the nuclear submarine, whose production fills the working hours of our life, can lead us to the despairing question, 'Is my life worth living?' It is therefore not so surprising that people who are praised by many for their successes and accomplishments often feel very unfulfilled, even to the point of committing suicide.

Boredom, resentment and depression are all sentiments of disconnectedness. They present life to us as a broken connection. They give us a sense of not-belonging. In interpersonal relations, this disconnectedness is experienced as loneliness. When we are lonely we perceive ourselves as isolated individuals surrounded, perhaps, by many people, but not really part of any supporting or nurturing community. Loneliness is without doubt one of the most widespread diseases of our time. It affects not only retired life but also family life, neighbourhood life, · school life and business life. It causes suffering not only in elderly people but also in children, teenagers and adults. It enters not only prisons but also private homes, office buildings and hospitals. It is even visible in the diminishing interaction between people on the streets of our cities. Out of all this pervading loneliness many cry, 'Is there anyone who really cares? Is there anyone who can take away my inner sense of isolation? Is there anyone with whom I can feel at home?'

It is this paralyzing sense of separation that constitutes the core of much human suffering. We can take a lot of physical and even mental pain when we know that it truly makes us a part of the life we live together in this world. But when we feel cut off from the human family, we quickly lose heart. As long as we believe that our pains and struggles connect us with our fellow men and women and thus make us part of the common human struggle for a better future, we are quite willing to accept a demanding task. But when we think of ourselves as passive bystanders who have no contribution to make to the story of life, our pains are no longer growing pains and our struggles no longer offer new life, because then we have a sense that our lives die out behind us and do not lead us anywhere. Sometimes, indeed, we have to say that the only thing we remember of our recent past is that we were very busy, that everything seemed very urgent, and that we could hardly get it all done. *What* we were doing we have forgotten. This shows how isolated we have become. The past no longer carries us to the future; it simply leaves us worried, without any promise that things will be different.

Our urge to be set free from this isolation can become so strong that it bursts forth in violence. Then our need for an intimate relationship – for a friend, a lover, or an appreciative community – turns into a desperate grabbing for anyone who offers some immediate satisfaction, some release of tension, or some temporary feeling of at-oneness. Then our need for each other degenerates into a dangerous aggression that causes much harm and only intensifies our feelings of loneliness.

CONCLUSION

I hope that these reflections have brought us a little closer to the meaning of the word *worry* as it was used by Jesus. Today worrying means to be occupied and preoccupied with many things, while at the same time being bored, resentful, depressed and very lonely. I am not trying to say that all of us are worried in such an extreme way all the time. Yet, there is little doubt in my mind that the experience of being filled yet unfulfilled touches most of us to some degree at some time. In our highly technological and competitive world, it is hard to avoid completely the forces which fill up our inner and outer space and disconnect us from our innermost selves, our fellow human beings, and our God.

One of the most notable characteristics of worrying is that it fragments our lives. The many things to do, to think about, to plan for, the many people to remember, to visit, or to talk with, the many causes to attack or defend, all these pull us apart and make us lose our centre. Worrying causes us to be 'all over the place,' but seldom at home. One way to express the spiritual

15

crisis of our time is to say that most of us have an address but cannot be found there. We know where we belong, but we keep being pulled away in many directions, as if we were still homeless. 'All these other things' keep demanding our attention. They lead us so far from home that we eventually forget our true address, that is, the place where we can be addressed.

Jesus responds to this condition of being filled yet unfulfilled, very busy yet unconnected, all over the place yet never at home. He wants to bring us to the place where we belong. But his call to live a spiritual life can only be heard when we are willing honestly to confess our own homeless and worrying existence and recognize its fragmenting effect on our daily life. Only then can a desire for our true home develop. It is of this desire that Jesus speaks when He says, 'Do not worry … Set your hearts on his kingdom first … and all these other things will be given you as well.'

'His Kingdom First'

INTRODUCTION

Jesus does not respond to our worry-filled way of living by saying that we should not be so busy with worldly affairs. He does
not try to pull us away from the many events, activities and people that make up our lives. He does not tell us that what we do
is unimportant, valueless or useless. Nor does He suggest that
we should withdraw from our involvements and live quiet, rest-
ful lives removed from the struggles of the world.

Jesus' response to our worry-filled lives is quite different. He
asks us to shift the point of gravity, to relocate the centre of
our attention, to change our priorities. Jesus wants us to move
from the 'many things' to the 'one necessary thing'. It is important for us to realize that Jesus in no way wants us to leave
our many-faceted world. Rather, He wants us to live in it, but
firmly rooted in the centre of all things. Jesus does not speak
about a change of activities, a change in contacts, or even a
change of pace. He speaks about a change of heart. This
change of heart makes everything different, even while everything appears to remain the same. This is the meaning of
'Set your hearts on his kingdom first … and all these other
things will be given you as well.' What counts is where our
hearts are. When we worry, we have our hearts in the wrong

place. Jesus asks us to move our hearts to the centre, where all other things fall into place.

What is this centre? Jesus calls it the kingdom, the kingdom of His Father. For us of the twentieth century, this may not have much meaning. Kings and kingdoms do not play an important role in our daily life. But only when we understand Jesus' words as an urgent call to make the life of God's Spirit our priority can we see better what is at stake. A heart set on the Father's kingdom is also a heart set on the spiritual life. To set our hearts on the kingdom therefore means to make the life of the Spirit within and among us the centre of all we think, say, or do.

I now want to explore in some depth this life in the Spirit. First we need to see how in Jesus' own life the Spirit of God manifests itself. Then we need to discern what it means for us to be called by Jesus to enter with Him into this life of the Spirit.

JESUS' LIFE

There is little doubt that Jesus' life was a very busy life. He was busy teaching His disciples, preaching to the crowds, healing the sick, exorcising demons, responding to questions from foes and friends, and moving from one place to another. Jesus was so involved in activities that it became difficult to have any time alone. The following story gives us the picture: 'They brought to him all who were sick and those who were possessed by devils. The whole town came crowding round the door, and he cured many who were suffering from diseases of one kind or another; he also cast out many devils … In the morning, long before dawn, he got up and left the house, and went off to a lonely place and prayed there. Simon and his companions set out in search of him, and when they found him they said, "Everybody is looking for you." He answered, "Let us go elsewhere, to the neighbouring country towns, so that I can preach there too, because that is why I came." And he went all through Galilee, preaching in their synagogues and casting out devils' (Mark 1:32–39).

It is clear from this account that Jesus had a very filled life and was seldom if ever left alone. He might even appear to us as a fanatic driven by a compulsion to get His message across at any cost. The truth, however, is different. The deeper we enter into the Gospel accounts of His life, the more we see that Jesus was not a zealot trying to accomplish many different things in order to reach a self-imposed goal. On the contrary, everything we know about Jesus indicates that He was concerned with only one thing: to do the will of His Father. Nothing in the Gospels is as impressive as Jesus' single-minded obedience to His Father. From His first recorded words in the Temple, 'Did you not know that I must be busy with my Father's affairs?' (Luke 2:49), to His last words on the cross, 'Father, into your hands I commit my spirit' (Luke 23:46), Jesus' only concern was to do the will of His Father. He says, 'The Son can do nothing by himself; he can do only what he sees the Father doing' (John 5:19). The works Jesus did are the works the Father sent Him to do, and the words He spoke are the words the Father gave him. He leaves no doubt about this: 'If I am not doing my Father's work, there is no need to believe me ...' (John 10:37); 'My word is not my own; it is the word of the one who sent me' (John 14:24).

Jesus is not our Saviour simply because of what He said to us or did for us. He is our Saviour because what He said and did was said and done in obedience to His Father. That is why St Paul could say, 'As by one man's disobedience many were made sinners, so by one man's obedience many will be made righteous' (Romans 5:19). Jesus is the obedient one. The centre of his life is this obedient relationship with the Father. This may be hard for us to understand, because the word *obedience* has so many negative connotations in our society. It makes us think of authority figures who impose their wills against our desires. It makes us remember unhappy childhood events or hard tasks performed under threats of punishment. But none of this applies to Jesus' obedience. His obedience means a total, fearless listening to His loving Father. Between the Father and the Son there is only love. Everything that belongs to the Father, He entrusts to the Son (Luke 10:22), and everything the Son has received, He returns to the Father. The Father opens Himself totally to the Son and puts everything in His hands: all knowledge (John 12:50), all glory (John 8:54), all power (John 5:19–21). And the Son opens Himself totally to the Father and thus returns everything into His Father's hands. 'I came from the Father and have come into the world and now I leave the world to go the Father' (John 16:28).

This inexhaustible love between the Father and the Son includes and yet transcends all forms of love known to us. It includes the love of a father and mother, a brother and sister, a husband and wife, a teacher and friend. But it also goes far beyond the many limited and limiting human experiences of love we know. It is a caring yet demanding love. It is a supportive yet severe love. It is a gentle yet strong love. It is a love that gives life yet accepts death. In this divine love Jesus was sent into the world, to this divine love Jesus offered himself on the cross. This all-embracing love, which epitomizes the relationship between the Father and the Son, is a divine Person, coequal with the Father and the Son. It has a personal name. It is called the Holy Spirit. The Father loves the Son and pours himself out in the Son. The Son is loved by the Father and returns all he is to the Father. The Spirit is love itself, eternally embracing the Father and the Son.

This eternal community of love is the centre and source of Jesus' spiritual life, a life of uninterrupted attentiveness to the

Father in the Spirit of love. It is from this life that Jesus' ministry grows. His eating and fasting, His praying and acting, His travelling and resting, His preaching and teaching, His exorcising and healing, were all done in this Spirit of love. We will never understand the full meaning of Jesus' richly varied ministry unless we see how the many things are rooted in the one thing: listening to the Father in the intimacy of perfect love. When we see this, we will also realize that the goal of Jesus' ministry is nothing less than to bring us into this most intimate community.

OUR LIVES

Our lives are destined to become like the life of Jesus. The whole purpose of Jesus' ministry is to bring us to the house of His Father. Not only did Jesus come to free us from the bonds of sin and death, He also came to lead us into the intimacy of His divine life. It is difficult for us to imagine what this means. We tend to emphasize the distance between Jesus and ourselves. We see Jesus as the all-knowing and all-powerful Son of God who is unreachable for us sinful, broken human beings. But in thinking this way, we forget that Jesus came to give us His own life. He came to lift us up into loving community with the Father. Only when we recognize the radical purpose of Jesus' ministry will we be able to understand the meaning of the spiritual life. Everything that belongs to Jesus is given for us to receive. All that Jesus does we may also do. Jesus does not speak about us as second-class citizens. He does not withhold anything from us: 'I have made known to you everything I have learned from my Father' (John 15:15); 'Whoever believes in me will perform the same works as I do myself' (John 14:12). Jesus wants us to be where He is. In His priestly prayer, He leaves no doubt about His intentions: 'Father, may they be one in us, as you are in me and I am in you ... I have given them the glory you gave to me, that they may be one as we are one. With me in them and you in me, may they be so completely one that the world will realize ... that I have loved them as much as you loved me. Father, I want those you have given me to be with me where I am, so that they may always see the glory you have given me ... I have made your name known to them and will continue to make it known, so that the love with which you loved me may be in them, and so that I may be in them' (John 17:21–26).

These words beautifully express the nature of Jesus' ministry. He became like us so that we might become like Him. He did not cling to His equality with God, but emptied Himself and became as we are so that we might become like Him and thus share in His divine life.

This radical transformation of our lives is the work of the Holy Spirit. The disciples could hardly comprehend what Jesus meant. As long as Jesus was present to them in the flesh, they did not yet recognize His full presence in the Spirit. That is why Jesus said: 'It is for your own good that I am going because unless I go, the Advocate [the Holy Spirit] will not come to you; but if I do go, I will send him to you ... When the Spirit of truth comes he will lead you to the complete truth, since he will not be speaking as from himself but will say only what he has learned; and he will tell you of the things to come. He will glorify me, since all he tells you will be taken from what is mine. Everything the Father has is mine; that is why I said: All he tells you will be taken from what is mine' (John 16:7, 13–15).

Jesus sends the Spirit so that we may be led to the full truth of the divine life. *Truth* does not mean an idea, concept or doctrine, but the true relationship. To be led into the truth is to be led into the same relationship that Jesus has with the Father; it is to enter into a divine betrothal.

Thus Pentecost is the completion of Jesus' mission. On Pentecost the fullness of Jesus' ministry becomes visible. When the Holy Spirit descends upon the disciples and dwells with them, their lives are transformed into Christ-like lives, lives shaped by the same love that exists between the Father and the Son. The spiritual life is indeed a life in which we are lifted up to become partakers of the divine love.

To be lifted up into the divine life of the Father, the Son, and the Holy Spirit does not mean, however, to be taken out of the world. On the contrary, those who have entered into the spiritual life are precisely the ones who are sent into the world to continue and fulfil the work that Jesus began. The spiritual life does not remove us from the world but leads us deeper into it. Jesus says to His Father, 'As you sent me into the world, I have sent them into the world' (John 17:18). He makes it clear that precisely because His disciples no longer belong to the world, they can live in the world as He did: 'I am not asking you to remove them from the world, but to protect them from the evil one. They do not belong to the world any more than I belong to the world' (John 17:15–16). Life in the Spirit of Jesus is therefore a life in which Jesus' coming into the world – His incarnation, His death and resurrection – is lived out by those who have entered into the same obedient relationship to the Father which marked Jesus' own life. Having become sons and daughters as Jesus was Son, our lives become a continuation of Jesus' mission.

'Being in the world without being of the world.' These words summarize well the way Jesus speaks of the spiritual life. It is a life in which we are totally transformed by the Spirit of love. Yet it is a life in which everything seems to remain the same. To live a spiritual life does not mean that we must leave our families, give up our jobs, or change our ways of working; it does not mean that we have to withdraw from social or political activities, or lose interest in literature and art; it does not require severe forms of asceticism or long hours of prayer. Changes such as these may in fact grow out of our spiritual life, and for some people radical decisions may be necessary. But the spiritual life can be lived in as many ways as there are people. What is new is that we have moved from the many things to the kingdom of God. What is new is that we are set free from the compulsions of our world and have set our hearts on the only necessary thing. What is new is that we no longer experience the many things, people, and events as endless causes for worry, but begin to experience them as the rich variety of ways in which God makes His presence known to us.

Indeed, living a spiritual life requires a change of heart, a conversion. Such a conversion may be marked by a sudden inner change, or it can take place through a long, quiet process of transformation. But it always involves an inner experience of oneness. We realize that we are in the centre, and that from there all that is and all that takes place can be seen and understood as part of the mystery of God's life with us. Our conflicts and pains, our tasks and promises, our families and friends, our activities and projects, our hopes and aspirations, no longer appear to us as a fatiguing variety of things which we can barely keep together, but rather as affirmations and revelations of the new life of the Spirit in us. 'All these other things', which so occupied and preoccupied us, now come as gifts or challenges that strengthen and deepen the new life which we have discovered. This does not mean that the spiritual life makes things easier or takes our struggles and pains away. The lives of Jesus' disciples clearly show that suffering does not diminish because of conversion. Sometimes it even becomes more intense. But our attention is no longer directed to the 'more or less'. What matters is to listen attentively to the Spirit and to go obediently where we are being led, whether to a joyful or a painful place.

Poverty, pain, struggle, anguish, agony, and even inner darkness may continue to be part of our experience. They may even be God's way of purifying us. But life is no longer boring, resentful, depressing, or lonely because we have come to know that everything that happens is part of our way to the house of the Father.

CONCLUSION

'His kingdom first'. I hope that these words have received some new meaning. They call us to follow Jesus on His obedient way, to enter with Him into the community established by the demanding love of the Father, and to live all of life from there. The kingdom is the place where God's Spirit guides us, heals us, challenges us, and renews us continuously. When our hearts are set on that kingdom, our worries will slowly move to the background, because the many things which made us worry so much start to fall into place. It is important to realize that 'setting your heart on the kingdom' is not a method for winning prizes. In that case the spiritual life would become like winning the jackpot on a TV game show. The words 'all other things will be given you as well' express that indeed God's love and care extend to our whole being. When we set our hearts on the life in the Spirit of Christ, we will come to see and understand better how God keeps us in the palm of His hand. We will come to be better understanding of what we truly need for our physical and mental well-being, and we will come to experience the intimate connections between our spiritual life and our temporal needs while journeying through His world.

But this leaves us with a very difficult question. Is there a way to move from our worry-filled life to the life of the Spirit? Must we simply wait passively until the Spirit comes along and blows away our worries? Are there any ways by which we can prepare ourselves for the life of the Spirit and deepen that life once it has touched us? The distance between the filled yet unfulfilled life on the one hand, and the spiritual life on the other, is so great that it may seem quite unrealistic to expect to move from one to another. The claims that daily living makes on us are so real, so immediate, and so urgent that a life in the Spirit seems beyond our capabilities.

My description of the worry-filled life and the spiritual life as the two extremes of the spectrum of living was necessary to make clear what is at stake. But most of us are neither worrying constantly nor absorbed solely in the Spirit. Often there are flashes of the presence of God's Spirit in the midst of our worries, and often worries arise even when we experience the life of the Spirit in our innermost self. It is important that we gradually realize where we are and learn how we can let the life of God's Spirit grow stronger in us.

This brings me to the final task: to describe the main disciplines which can support us in our desire to have our worries lose their grip on us, and to let the Spirit guide us to the true freedom of the children of God.

'Set Your Hearts'

3

INTRODUCTION

The spiritual life is a gift. It is the gift of the Holy Spirit, who lifts us up into the kingdom of God's love. But to say that being lifted up into the kingdom of love is a divine gift does not mean that we wait passively until the gift is offered to us. Jesus tells us to set our hearts on the kingdom. Setting our hearts on something involves not only serious aspiration but also strong determination. A spiritual life requires human effort. The forces that keep pulling us back into a worry-filled life are far from easy to overcome. 'How hard it is,' Jesus exclaims, '... to enter the kingdom of God!' (Mark 10:23). And to convince us of the need for hard work, He says, 'If anyone wants to be a follower of mine, let him renounce himself and take up his cross and follow me' (Matthew 16:24).

Here we touch the question of discipline in the spiritual life. A spiritual life without discipline is impossible. Discipline is the other side of discipleship. The practice of a spiritual discipline makes us more sensitive to the small, gentle voice of God. The prophet Elijah did not encounter God in the mighty wind or in the earthquake or in the fire, but in the small voice (see 1 Kings 19:9–13). Through the practice of a spiritual discipline we become attentive to that small voice and willing to respond when we hear it.

From all that I said about our worried, over-filled lives, it is clear that we are usually surrounded by so much inner and outer noise that it is hard to truly hear our God when He is speaking to us. We have often become deaf, unable to know when God calls us and unable to understand in which direction He calls us. Thus our lives have become absurd. In the word *absurd* we find the Latin word *surdus*, which means 'deaf'. A spiritual life requires discipline because we need to learn to listen to God, who constantly speaks but whom we seldom hear. When, however, we learn to listen, our lives become obedient lives. The word *obedient* comes from the Latin word *audire*, which means 'listening'. A spiritual discipline is necessary in order to move slowly from an absurd to an obedient life, from a life filled with noisy worries to a life in which there is some free inner space where we can listen to our God and follow His guidance. Jesus' life was a life of obedience. He was always listening to the Father, always attentive to His voice, always alert for His directions. Jesus was 'all ears'. That is true prayer: being all ears for God. The core of all prayer is indeed listening, obediently standing in the presence of God.

A spiritual discipline, therefore, is the concentrated effort to create some inner and outer space in our lives, where this obedience can be practised. Through a spiritual discipline we prevent the world from filling our lives to such an extent that there is no place left to listen. A spiritual discipline sets us free to pray or, to say it better, allows the Spirit of God to pray in us.

I will now present two disciplines through which we can 'set our hearts on the kingdom'. They can be considered as disciplines of prayer. They are the discipline of solitude and the discipline of community.

SOLITUDE

Without solitude it is virtually impossible to live a spiritual life. Solitude begins with a time and place for God, and Him alone. If we really believe not only that God exists but also that He is actively present in our lives – healing, teaching and guiding – we need to set aside a time and space to give Him our undivided attention. Jesus says, 'Go to your private room and, when you have shut the door, pray to your Father who is in that secret place' (Matthew 6:6).

To bring some solitude into our lives is one of the most necessary but also most difficult disciplines. Even though we may have a deep desire for real solitude, we also experience a certain apprehension as we approach that solitary place and time. As soon as we are alone, without people to talk with, books to read, TV to watch, or phone calls to make, an inner chaos opens up in us. This chaos can be so disturbing and so confusing that we can hardly wait to get busy again. Entering a private room and shutting the door, therefore, does not mean that we immediately shut out all our inner doubts, anxieties, fears, bad memories, unresolved conflicts, angry feelings and impulsive desires. On the contrary, when we have removed our outer distractions, we often find that our inner distractions manifest themselves to us in full force. We often use the outer distractions to shield ourselves from the interior noises. It is thus not surprising that we have a difficult time being alone. The confrontation with our inner conflicts can be too painful for us to endure.

This makes the discipline of solitude all the more important. Solitude is not a spontaneous response to an occupied and preoccupied life. There are too many reasons not to be alone. Therefore we must begin by carefully planning some solitude. Five or ten minutes a day may be all we can tolerate. Perhaps we are ready for an hour every day, an afternoon every week, a day every month, or a week every year. The amount of time will vary for each person according to temperament, age, job, lifestyle and maturity. But we do not take the spiritual life seriously if we do not set aside some time to be with God and listen to Him. We may have to write it in black and white in our daily calendar so that nobody else can take away this period of time. Then we will be able to say to our friends, neighbours, students, customers, clients or patients, 'I'm sorry, but I've already made an appointment at that time and it can't be changed'.

Once we have committed ourselves to spending time in solitude, we develop an attentiveness to God's voice in us. In the beginning, during the first days, weeks, or even months, we may have the feeling that we are simply wasting our time. Time in solitude may at first seem little more than a time in which we are bombarded by thousands of thoughts and feelings that emerge from hidden areas of our mind. One of the early Christian writers describes the first stage of solitary prayer as the experience of a man who, after years of living with open doors, suddenly decides to shut them. The visitors who used to come and enter his home start pounding on his doors, wondering why they are not allowed to enter. Only when they realize that they are not welcome do they gradually stop coming. This is the experience of anyone who decides to enter into solitude after a life without much spiritual discipline. At first, the many distractions keep presenting themselves. Later, as they receive less and less attention, they slowly withdraw.

It is clear that what matters is faithfulness to the discipline. In the beginning, solitude seems so contrary to our desires that we are constantly tempted to run away from it. One way of running away is daydreaming or simply falling asleep. But when we stick to our discipline, in the conviction that God is with us even when we do not yet hear Him, we slowly discover that we do not want to miss our time alone with God. Although we do not experience much satisfaction in our solitude, we realize that a day without solitude is less 'spiritual' than a day with it.

Intuitively, we know that it is important to spend time in solitude. We even start looking forward to this strange period of uselessness. This desire for solitude is often the first sign of prayer, the first indication that the presence of God's Spirit no longer remains unnoticed. As we empty ourselves of our many worries, we come to know not only with our mind but also with our heart that we never were really alone, that God's Spirit was with us all along. Thus we come to understand what Paul writes to the Romans, 'Sufferings bring patience … and patience brings perseverance, and perseverance brings hope, and this hope is not deceptive, because the love of God has been poured into our hearts by the Holy Spirit which has been given to us' (Romans 5:4–6). In solitude, we come to know the Spirit who has already been given to us. The pains and struggles we encounter in our solitude thus become the way to hope, because our hope is not based on something that will happen after our sufferings are over, but on the real presence of God's healing Spirit in the midst of these sufferings. The discipline of solitude allows us gradually to come in touch with this hopeful presence of God in our lives, and allows us also to taste even now the beginnings of the joy and peace which belong to the new heaven and the new earth.

The discipline of solitude, as I have described it here, is one of the most powerful disciplines in developing a prayerful life. It is a simple, though not easy, way to free us from the slavery of our occupations and preoccupations and to begin to hear the voice that makes all things new.

Let me give a more concrete description of how the discipline of solitude may be practised. It is a great advantage to have a room or a corner of a room – or a large closet! – reserved for the discipline of solitude. Such a 'ready' place helps us set our hearts on the kingdom without time-consuming preparations. Some

31

people like to decorate such a place with an icon, a candle, or a simple plant. But the important thing is that the place of solitude remains a simple, uncluttered place. There we dwell in the presence of the Lord. Our temptation is to do something useful: to read something stimulating, to think about something interesting, or to experience something unusual. But our moment of solitude is precisely a moment in which we want to be in the presence of our Lord with empty hands, naked, vulnerable, useless, without much to show, prove, or defend. That is how we slowly learn to listen to God's small voice. But what to do with our many distractions? Should we fight these distractions and hope that thus we will become more attentive to God's voice? This does not seem the way to come to prayer. Creating an empty space where we can listen to God's Spirit is not easy when we are putting all our energy into fighting distractions. By fighting distractions in such a direct way, we end up paying more attention to them than they deserve. We have, however, the words of Scripture to which to pay attention. A psalm, a parable, a biblical story, a saying of Jesus, or a word of Paul, Peter, James, Jude or John can help us to focus our attention on God's presence. Thus we deprive those 'many other things' of their power over us. When we place words from the Scriptures in the centre of our solitude, such words – whether a short expression, a few sentences, or a longer text – can function as the point to which we return when we have wandered off in different directions. They form a safe anchoring place in a stormy sea. At the end of such a period of quiet dwelling with God we may, through intercessory prayer, lead all the people who are part of our lives, friends as well as enemies, into his healing presence. And why not conclude with the words that Jesus Himself taught us: the Our Father?

This is only one specific form in which the discipline of solitude may be practised. Endless variations are possible. Walks in nature, the repetition of short prayers such as the Jesus Prayer, simple forms of chanting, certain movements or postures – these and many other elements can become a helpful part of the discipline of solitude. But we have to decide which particular form of this discipline best fits us, to which we can remain faithful. It is better to have a daily practice of ten minutes' solitude than to have a whole hour once in a while. It is better to become familiar with one posture than to keep experimenting with different ones. Simplicity and regularity are the best guides in finding our way. They allow us to make the discipline of solitude as much part of our daily lives as eating and sleeping. When that happens, our noisy worries will slowly lose their power over us and the renewing activity of God's Spirit will slowly make its presence known.

Although the discipline of solitude asks us to set aside time and space, what finally matters is that our hearts become like quiet cells where God can dwell, wherever we go and whatever we do. The more we train ourselves to spend time with God and Him alone, the more we will discover that God is with us at all times and in all places. Then we will be able to recognize Him even in the midst of a busy and active life. Once the solitude of time and space has become a solitude of the heart, we will never have to leave that solitude. We will be able to live the spiritual life in any place and any time. Thus the discipline of solitude enables us to live active lives in the world, while remaining always in the presence of the living God.

COMMUNITY

The discipline of solitude does not stand alone. It is intimately related to the discipline of community. Community as discipline is the effort to create a free and empty space among people where together we can practice true obedience. Through the discipline of community we prevent ourselves from clinging to each other in fear and loneliness, and clear free space to listen to the liberating voice of God.

It may sound strange to speak of community as discipline, but without discipline community becomes a 'soft' word, referring more to a safe, homey, and exclusive place than to the space where new life can be received and brought to its fullness. Wherever true community presents itself, discipline is crucial. It is crucial not only in the many old and new forms of the common life but also in the sustaining relationships of friendship, marriage and family. To create space for God among us requires the constant recognition of the Spirit of God in each other. When we have come to know the life-giving Spirit of God in the centre of our solitude and have thus been able to affirm our true identity, we can also see that same life-giving Spirit speaking to us through our fellow human beings. And when we have come to recognize the life-giving Spirit of God as the source of our life together, we too will more readily hear His voice in our solitude.

Friendship, marriage, family, religious life, and every other form of community is solitude greeting solitude, spirit speaking to spirit, and heart calling to heart. It is the grateful recognition of God's call to share life together and the joyful offering of a hospitable space where the recreating power of God's Spirit can become manifest. Thus all forms of life together can become ways to reveal to each other the real presence of God in our midst.

Community has little to do with mutual compatibility. Similarities in educational background, psychological make-up, or social status can bring us together, but they can never be the basis for community. Community is grounded in God, who calls us together, and not in the attractiveness of people to each other. There are many groups that have been formed to protect their own interests, to defend their own status, or to promote their own causes, but none of these is a Christian community. Instead of breaking through the walls of fear and creating new space for God, they close themselves to real or imaginary intruders. The mystery of community is precisely that it embraces *all* people, whatever their individual differences may be, and allows them to live together as brothers and sisters of Christ and sons and daughters of His heavenly Father.

I would like to describe one concrete form of this discipline of community. It is the practice of listening together. In our wordy world we usually spend our time together talking. We feel most comfortable in sharing experiences, discussing interesting subjects, or arguing about current issues. It is through a very active verbal exchange that we try to discover each other. But often we find that words function more as walls than as gates, more as ways to keep distance than to come close. Often – even against our own desires – we find ourselves competing with each other. We try to prove to each other that we are worth being paid attention to, that we have something to show that makes us special. The discipline of community helps us to be silent together. This disciplined silence is not an embarrassing silence, but a silence in which together we pay attention to the Lord who calls us together. In this way we come to know each other not as people who cling anxiously to our self-constructed identity, but as people who are loved by the same God in a very intimate and unique way.

Here – as with the discipline of solitude – it is often the words of Scripture that can lead us into this communal silence. Faith, as Paul says, comes from hearing. We have to hear the word from each other. When we come together from different geographical, historical, psychological and religious directions, listening to the same word spoken by different people can create in us a common openness and vulnerability that allow us to recognize that we are safe together in that word. Thus we can come to discover our true identity as a community, thus we can come to experience what it means to be called together, and thus we can recognize that the same Lord whom we discovered in our solitude also speaks in the solitude of our neighbours, whatever their language, denomination or character. In this listening together to the word of God, a true creative silence can grow. This silence is a silence filled with the caring presence of God. Thus listening together to the word can free us from our competition and rivalry and allow us to recognize our true identity as sons and daughters of the same loving God and brothers and sisters of our Lord Jesus Christ, and thus of each other.

This example of the discipline of community is one out of many. Celebrating together, working together, playing together – these are all ways in which the discipline of community can be practised. But whatever its concrete shape or form, the discipline of community always points us beyond the boundaries of race, sex, nationality, character, or age, and always reveals to us who we are before God and for each other.

The discipline of community makes us persons; that is, people who are sounding through to each other (the Latin word *personare* means 'sounding through') a truth, a beauty, and a love which is greater, fuller, and richer than we ourselves can grasp. In true community we are windows constantly offering each other new views on the mystery of God's presence in our lives. Thus the discipline of community is a true discipline of prayer. It makes us alert to the presence of the Spirit who cries out 'Abba', Father, among us and thus prays from the centre of our common life. Community thus is obedience practised together. The question is not simply, 'Where does God lead me as an individual person who tries to do His will?' More basic and more significant is the question, 'Where does God lead us as a people?' This question requires that we pay careful attention to

God's guidance in our life together and that together we search for a creative response. Here we come to see how prayer and action are indeed one, because whatever we do as a community can only be an act of true obedience when it is a response to the way we have heard God's voice in our midst.

Finally, we have to keep in mind that community, like solitude, is primarily a quality of the heart. While it remains true that we will never know what community is if we never come together in one place, community does not necessarily mean being physically together. We can well live in community while being physically alone. In such a situation, we can act freely, speak honestly, and suffer patiently, because of the intimate bond of love that unites us with others even when time and place separate us from them. The community of love stretches out not only beyond the boundaries of countries and continents but also beyond the boundaries of decades and centuries. Not only the awareness of those who are far away but also the memory of those who lived long ago can lead us into a healing, sustaining, and guiding community. The space for God in community transcends all limits of time and place.

Thus the discipline of community frees us to go wherever the Spirit guides us, even to places we would rather not go. This is the real Pentecost experience. When the Spirit descended on the disciples huddling together in fear, they were set free to move out of their closed room into the world. As long as they were assembled in fear they did not yet form community. But when they had received the Spirit, they became a body of free people who could stay in communion with each other even when they were as far from each other as Rome is from Jerusalem. Thus, when it is the Spirit of God and not fear that unites us in community, no distance of time or place can separate us.

CONCLUSION

Through the discipline of solitude we discover space for God in our innermost being. Through the discipline of community we discover a place for God in our life together. Both disciplines belong together precisely because the space within us and the space among us are the same space.

It is in that divine space that God's Spirit prays in us. Prayer is first and foremost the active presence of the Holy Spirit in our personal and communal lives. Through the disciplines of solitude and community we try to remove – slowly, gently, yet persistently – the many obstacles which prevent us from listening to God's voice within us. God speaks to us not only once in a while but always. Day and night, during work and during play, in joy and in sorrow, God's Spirit is actively present in us. Our task is to allow that presence to become real for us in all we do, say, or think. Solitude and community are the disciplines by which the space becomes free for us to listen to the presence of God's Spirit and to respond fearlessly and generously. When we have heard God's voice in our solitude we will also hear it in our life together. When we have heard Him in our fellow human beings, we will also hear Him when we are with Him alone. Whether in solitude or community, whether alone or with others, we are called to live obedient lives, that is, lives of unceasing prayer – 'unceasing' not because of the many prayers we say but because of our alertness to the unceasing prayer of God's Spirit within and among us.

Conclusion

My original questions were, 'What does it mean to live a spiritual life?' and 'How do we live it?' In this book I have described the spiritual life as the active presence of God's Spirit in the midst of a worry-filled existence. This life becomes a possibility when, by the disciplines of solitude and community, we slowly create some free inner space in our filled lives and so allow God's Spirit to become manifest to us.

We live in a worry-filled world. We find ourselves occupied and preoccupied with many things, while at the same time feeling bored, resentful, depressed and very lonely. In the midst of this world the Son of God, Jesus Christ, appears and offers us new life, the life of the Spirit of God. We desire this life, but we also realize it is so radically different from what we are used to that even aspiring to it seems unrealistic. How, then, can we move from fragmentation to unity, from many things to the one necessary thing, from our divided lives to undivided lives in the Spirit? A hard struggle is required. It is the struggle to allow God's Spirit to work in us and recreate us. But this struggle is not beyond our strength. It calls for some very specific, well-planned steps. It calls for a few moments a day in the presence of God when we can listen to His voice precisely in the midst of our many concerns. It also calls for the persistent endeavour to be with others in a new way by seeing them not as people to whom we can cling in fear, but as fellow human beings with whom we can create new space for God. These well-planned steps, these disciplines, are the concrete ways of 'setting your hearts on his kingdom', and they can slowly dismantle the power of our worries and thus lead us to unceasing prayer.

The beginning of the spiritual life is often difficult not only because the powers which cause us to worry are so strong but also because the presence of God's Spirit seems barely noticeable. If, however, we are faithful to our disciplines, a new hunger will make itself known. This new hunger is the first sign of God's presence. When we remain attentive to this divine presence, we will be led always deeper into the kingdom. There, to our joyful surprise, we will discover that all things are being made new.

INTIMACY

ॐ

To John Eudes

Acknowledgments

This book is born out of a two-year 'visit' to the University of Notre Dame. The many friendships with students and teachers made it very easy for me to overcome the feeling of being a guest and to fully participate in the intense life of this fast-developing campus, which not only reflects but also stimulates the many turbulent changes in feelings, thoughts and actions of modern society.

Without the stimulation and support of many students the following chapters never would have been written. Special thanks are due to Frank Allman, Ray Novaco, Dwight Norwood, Bob Bradley, Joe Ahearn, Mike McCarty, Greg Milmoe and Joseph Wissink, who by their honest reactions, criticisms and corrections helped me to think and rethink, to write and rewrite.

In the preparation of the chapters about the ministry I found great help in the lively discussions with the Holy Cross priests of the University of Notre Dame. In particular I am grateful to Louis Putz, Joe Hoffmann, Joe Simons, David Burrell, John Gerber, Ralph Dunn, Jim Burtchaell, John Dunne, Claude Pomerleau and Don McNeill. By their great sympathy they made me part of their life and community and in many ways tuned me into the different problems of the priest on campus.

I also would like to express my great thankfulness to the many faculty members and their wives who encouraged me to write and took away the hesitancies of the foreigner in me. John and Mary Alice Santos, Don and Christine Costello, John and Martha Borkowski, and Charles and Carol Allen, offered through their friendship many insights which are expressed in the following pages.

I owe much to Joe Collins for his careful revisions of the manuscript.

Finally, I am grateful to Linda Papas and Mrs M. J. van der Meer for their secretarial work.

This book is dedicated to John Eudes Bamberger, monk and psychiatrist, eminent guide through the complexities of the inner life.

Contents

Introduction

The sources of the following chapters are many: teaching, counselling, discussing, chatting, partying, celebrating, and most of
all just being around. Each chapter is written because someone
– a student, a teacher, a minister, a priest, a religious brother or
sister – asked a question. I wrote on different occasions, for different people, with different questions in mind. I wrote not to
solve a problem or to formulate a theory but to respond to men
and women who wanted to share their struggles in trying to find
their vocation in this chaotic world.

Looking back on the variety of questions and concerns that
confronted me, I saw a unity in the many subjects that justifies
bringing them together in one book. First of all, there is a unity
of perspective, which is pastoral. Although the language and the
approach might be considered psychological, the perspective is
that of a priest who wonders how to understand what he sees
in the light of God's work with people, Secondly, there is a
unifying theme. It has become increasingly clear to me that
underlying the many concerns there was one main question:
'How can I find a creative and fulfilling intimacy in my relationship with God and my fellow human beings?' How can one
person develop a fruitful intimacy with another person? What
does intimacy mean in the life of a celibate priest or in a

community of religious? How can we be intimate with God during moments of celebration or silent prayer?

It is not surprising that many of these questions are raised in a university milieu, dominated by young adults. Erik Erikson has stressed how the careful balance between intimacy and distance is the most crucial psychological task of those coming out of their adolescence and trying to develop lasting and productive relationships. Today, however, the struggle for intimacy is no longer limited to one age group. In the midst of a competitive and demanding world, people of all ages have become painfully aware of their deep-seated desire for a place of intimacy. This desire is felt as much by married people and by priests and religious committed to a celibate life as it is by dating students.

Therefore this book can be considered a book about the inner life. It does not deal with the burning issues that have become such a real part of our daily life: inflation, unemployment, crime, hunger, poverty and the threat of nuclear war. But it tries to address itself directly to what seems to pervade all these problems to some degree: people's seldom articulated and often unrecognized desire for a real home in this world. For that reason, I would like to call this a book about intimacy.

The Context

꒳

1

From Magic to Faith

RELIGIOUS GROWTH IN PSYCHOLOGICAL PERSPECTIVE

During the year we are exposed to many events, trivial and significant, which usually don't raise questions unless we pay some special attention to them:

A paratrooper, Captain Ridgway, rowed from Cape Cod to Ireland with his friend. Overwhelmed by the greatness of the ocean and the incredible forces of nature, he found that the medal given to him by the Cape Codders kept him together and gave him words to pray.

One priest, smiling, said to another priest as they left a packed college church at the end of the semester, 'The finals are the best proof that man is basically religious.'

Little Johnny says, 'Hey, Dad, you can't make President Kennedy alive. But God can, can't He? Cause He can do everything!' And we think: 'Isn't little Johnny cute?'

You read about an astronaut, symbol of modern science, smuggling a cross into orbit, and you just don't know what to think about it.

Or you meet a student, coming from a deeply religious family where God was the source of strength and happiness, suddenly asking questions so deep and fundamental that everything that had happened before seems completely irrelevant to him.

Then you read about a group of young men leaving their good jobs, their comfortable homes and sometimes even their families to go to the most desperate places of this world, to live with people they don't even as yet know.

What about all this? Magic or Faith? Superstition or contact with ultimate reality? Something to avoid or to aspire to? To clarify these questions let us look at the life of a man from the time he is folded in the safe womb of his mother to the moment he is walking around, broad-shouldered, with his thumbs pushed behind his leather belt, curiously looking around at this world and what lies beyond. We will call this trip 'from Magic to Faith'. We all make this trip, and it might be worthwhile to look at it from a distance.

In each phase of a man's life we will stress one particular aspect of our development which is a constituent of a mature religious sentiment.

[a] The first five years of life

During the first five years of life we have to take three big steps out of the magical world in which we are born.

1. During the first 18 months we come to the somewhat frustrating discovery that we are not the centre of the world.

Most of you will agree that there are people and things outside of us which will continue to exist even when we don't. This is, however, not so self-evident as it seems. It is only through a long and often frustrating experience that we are able to discover the objective world. As a baby in the mother's womb, everything is there for us; mother is a part of ourself. Later, it can be quite a painful experience to discover that our cry does not create the milk, that our smile does not produce the mother, that our needs do not evoke their own satisfaction. Only gradually do we discover our mother as the other, as not just a part of ourself. Every time we experience that we are not ruling the world by our feelings, thoughts and actions, we are forced to realize that there are other persons, things and events which have their autonomy.

Therefore, the first step out of the magical world is the discovery of an objective reality. It can happen that we reach this objectivity only partially. Although we slowly unfold and become able to stand on our own feet and point to the things around us as objective realities available for our curious mind, this may not happen so easily in the religious dimension. Many mature, successful men in this life often might still treat God as part of themselves. God is the factotum which comes in handy in times of illness, shock, final exams, in every situation in which we feel insecure. And if it does not work, the only reaction may be to cry louder. Far from becoming the Other, whose existence does not depend on mine, He might remain the easy frame which fits best around the edges of my security. Great anxiety, caused by internal or external storms, can sometimes force us to regress to this level of religion. This regression may even save our life, as it did Captain Ridgway's. It gives us something to hold on to, a medal or a candle which can keep us together. It may be a very helpful form of religion; but certainly it is not a mature form of religion.

2. The second step out of our magical world is the formation of the language. Somewhere between our 18th month of life and our 3rd birthday we started mumbling our first sounds which slowly developed into words, sentences, and a language. Although it may be disappointing that there are things around us which do not belong to us, by words we can take revenge, because our first words give us a mysterious power over things. Like an American who is excited to discover that his first French

word, *garçon*, really brings the waiter to his table, the child experiences not so much the mastery of words but mastery of objects. It takes quite a while before we can detach the word from the object and give it a symbolic function.

The magical word gives us power not only over objects but also over our own instinctual impulses. Before we had words we couldn't resist the temptation of grabbing flowers in daddy's garden. But by the word 'flower' we became able to substitute the act of grabbing and touching, and with our hands clasped together at our back we could then say: 'nice flower, no touch'.[1]

Well, religion is full of words. Long litanies, exclamations and often-repeated formulas play a very important role in many religions. What concerns us here is that this use of words often does not transcend the magical phase. Instead of being the free and creative expression of deep realities communicable to our fellow man, the words may become a substitute for reality, a subtle form of power over the capricious movements of our gods, our devils, or our own impulses.

Is there not something of this magical world left in us if we feel that we will be saved if we say our prayers every day, or if we at least keep the custom of the three Hail Marys before going to bed? It seems difficult to overcome this word-magic. We feel pretty good if we have fulfilled our obligation, mumbled our table prayers, raced through our rosary or recited our breviary. We seem to be saying, 'God cannot do anything to us now. We did what He asked us to do, and now it is His turn to pay us back.' Our prayers give us some power over God, instead of engaging us in a real dialogue.

3. The third step out of the magical world is the formation of our conscience. This is the great event between our third and

---

[1] Selma H. Fraiberg, *The Magic Years* (Charles Scribner's Sons: 1959).

fifth years. When we had learned that objects existed outside ourselves which kept existing even if we did not, and when we had experienced that words were not omnipotent tools to manipulate the world around us, we were still confronted with a much more important step: the step from daddy to us. 'I am not going to hit my nasty little sister, not because Daddy does not like that, but because I don't like it, because it is bad.' The external disciplinary agent, daddy, mummy, priest etc., slowly is converted into an internal policeman.

Conscience becomes possible by the process of identification. We develop the capacity to interiorize certain aspects of the personality of another person, to make them a part of ourselves. In the case of moral development, we take over judgments, standards and values of beloved persons and incorporate them into our own personality.

Or is there something else happening at the same time? During those first four years of life we felt that daddy could do everything, that he was omnipotent, that he could solve all the problems and lift all the weights. In our fantasy, daddy is the greatest athlete in the world, he builds houses, writes books, creates bicycles and is able to get everything for me, if only he wants to. Well, we became disappointed sooner or later. Daddy turns out to be a square, after all. We couldn't really depend on him any longer. How could we solve this problem?

Interiorization might not solve the whole problem. The need for an omnipotent Father who gives us love, shelter and protection, in whose arms we can hide and feel safe, might simply be too intense. The magical father couldn't be done without, we needed him too much, and therefore, he stayed with us in another name: GOD. And so we thought that if daddy could not make President Kennedy live again, at least God could do it.

When Sigmund Freud wrote his *Future of an Illusion*, he irritated and deeply disturbed the faithful, by saying that religion is the continuation of infantile life and that God is the projection of the ever-present desire for shelter.

Freud's task was to cure people, that is, to make them become more mature. And looking at the many people in his office in Vienna who suffered from their religion more than they were saved by it, he tried to unmask their projections. The psychiatrist Rümke summarizes Freud's position when he writes: 'When man matures completely he realizes that his God image, often a father-God image, is a reincarnation of the infantile worldly father, loved and feared. God is apparently no more than a projection. If that which blocks his growth is taken away, the image fades. Man distinguishes good from evil according to his own standards. He has conquered the remainder of his neurosis, which was all that his religion was.'[2] What is important in this context is that Freud was not altogether wrong. We often stay in this magical and infantile world in which God is as nice to have around as the comforting blanket of Linus in 'Peanuts'. For many, religion is really not very much more than Freud found it to be, and for all of us, so many of our religious experiences are clothed in images of childhood that it is often very difficult to say where our infantilism ends and our religion begins.

It seems appropriate here to ask a critical question: Is the idea of God an infantile prolongation of our ideal father image, or is our receptivity to the child-father idea the result of our more profound and primary relationship with God? Indeed the basic criticism of Freud proposed by the German psychiatrist Binswanger is a reversal: God is not the prolongation of the child's relationship with his dad, but the child's feeling for his dad is a concretizing of an idea born of his most fundamental relation to his Creator. In other words, we couldn't love our

2 H. C. Rümke, *The Psychology of Unbelief* (Sheed & Ward: 1962).

father if God had not loved us first. But here we have left the field of psychology.[3]

In one way we have to agree with Freud: in so far as our God is a pure surrogate for our conscience and a preventative to the development of a rational mind, a mature self and an autonomous individual, it is only a sign of good health and insight to throw our God out as a disease called neurosis. It is even sad to notice how few have the courage to do this.

Healthy development means a gradual movement out of the magical world. Even when the development takes place in other areas, our religion easily remains on this immature level. In that case, God remains the magical pacifier whose existence depends on ours. Prayers remain tools to manipulate Him in our direction and religion is nothing more than a big, soft bed on which we doze away and deny the hardships of life. Our religious sentiment will never be mature 1) if God is not the Other, 2) if prayer is not a dialogue, and 3) if religion is not a source of creative autonomy.

[b] School age: 5–12 years

When we were about five years old we went to school. In the small unit of our family the most essential behavioural patterns were pretty well established. Our first experiences of trust, happiness, fear, friendship, joy and disappointment and our first reactions to these experiences took place in our parental home. But then we entered a new world. In school we met other boys and girls who also had parents and homes, and then we had to find out if what we learned at home really worked. In many ways our years in grade school were years in which our major patterns of behaviour were fortified, modified, enlarged or

[3] H. C. Rümke, *ibid*.

56

disrupted, years in which we experienced success and failure in a larger society than we were used to during the first years of our lives.

Religion in our society is generally a private affair. As soon as we heard about the new maths, the history of man, as soon as we learned how to do things ourselves and how to be master of our world, the chance was great that religion became isolated as a separate reality, good for Sunday and the pious hour of the week but not really related to all the new things we heard about this and other worlds. Allport says maturity comes only when a growing intelligence somehow is animated by the desire not to suffer arrested development, but to keep pace with the intake of relevant experience. 'In many people, so far as the religious sentiment is concerned, this inner demand is absent. Finding their childhood religion to have comforting value and lacking outside pressure, they cling to an essentially juvenile formulation.'[4]

A mature religion is integral in nature – that means that it is flexible enough to integrate all new knowledge within its frame of reference and keep pace with all the new discoveries of the human mind. It indeed takes the cross into the space craft. Going to school means starting on the road to science, and if religion does not follow the same road with an open and critical eye, the grown man who flies the ocean in superjets might be religiously still content with his tricycle. Essential for mature religion is the constant willingness to shift gears, to integrate new insights and to revise our positions.

[c] Adolescence: 12–18 years

With adolescence, we entered into a new and very critical phase of our development. Some of us might have experienced a

---

[4] Gordon Allport, *The Individual and his Religion* (Macmillan: 1950).

sudden and dramatic change, others gradually entered the new realities hardly noticing the entry.

Suddenly or gradually, we were confronted with the fact that not only is life outside of us very complicated but life inside of us is just as complicated, or even more so. Until this time we were very curious about all the things going on around us, were excited by all the new things we saw and heard; but then we sensed deep and, often, very strange and disturbing feelings inside. New, often dark, urges seemed to push us without our understanding. We were overwhelmed by feelings of intense joy and happiness, so much so that we didn't know what it meant. Or we were victims of a wish to die, to kill, to hurt, to destroy. We felt that we were torn apart sometimes by the most conflicting feelings and ideas; love and hate, desire to embrace and desire to kill; desire to give and desire to take.

Perhaps we touch here one of the most important crossroads of our religious development. The question is: can we accept and understand our inner conflicts in such a way that by clarification and understanding they become a source of maturation of our religious sentiment? Very often we fail. Very often religion has become identified with cleanliness, purity, the perfect life – and every feeling which seems to throw black spots on our white sheet seems to be antireligious. In that case we cannot allow ourselves to have strong sexual urges and cruel fantasies and aggressive desires. Religion says: 'No!' Do not curse, do not steal, do not kill, do not masturbate, do not gossip, do not, do not, do not... Then teachers who tell us to be nice, obedient and lovable start to irritate us no end. Nobody really seems to understand this strange new world of internal feelings which make us feel solemnly unique but, at the same time, horribly lonely.

Many of us remember how deeply we wanted understanding, how difficult it was to express ourselves and how few people really were close to us. A feeling of shame and guilt often made us feel terribly lonely and we felt that we were hypocrites whom nobody would love if they really knew how we felt. Many things are possible in this period. We might feel that religion was so oppressive and depressive, so far away from all our experience, so authoritarian and negativistic that the only way of resolving the conflict was to break away from it. Some became sick of the shouting priest in the pulpit, others never felt any understanding for their disturbing feelings or could no longer stand the obvious hypocrisy of many churchgoers, and many dropped away – some slowly, others in open rebellion.

But there is another reaction, perhaps more harmful. This is the tendency to deny and repress drastically the other side, the dark wishes, the unwelcome shadow. Then we are saying, 'After all, we are clean, pure, sinless, and we want to keep our record spotless.' We want to stay in complete control of ourselves, never have an evil thought, never curse, never get drunk, never fail, but always remain perfect, saintly and, in a way, so self-content that we don't leave anything to God to be saved. We walk through life as if we had swallowed an Easter candle, rigid and tense, always afraid that things will get out of hand.

This reaction is just as harmful as open rebellion, or even more so, because it blocks our way to religious maturity. But there is a way to maturity in which we can say, 'Yes, I have weak spots but that does not make me weak. I have ugly thoughts but that does not make me ugly.' This is the realization that we have to tolerate the weeds in order to have good wheat. If we try to eradicate all the weeds we might also pull out the precious wheat. A man who is never mad nor angry can never be passionately in favour of anything either. A man who never loses his temper might have nothing worthwhile to lose after all; he who is never down seldom enjoys himself either. He who never takes a risk might never fail, but he also will never succeed.

It is very difficult for each of us to believe in Christ's words, 'I did not come to call the virtuous, but sinners...' Perhaps no psychologist has stressed the need of self-acceptance as the way to self-realization so much as Carl Jung. For Jung, self-realization meant the integration of the shadow. It is the growing ability to allow the dark side of our personality to enter into our awareness and thus prevent a one-sided life in which only that which is presentable to the outside world is considered as a real part of ourselves. To come to an inner unity, totality and wholeness, every part of our self should be accepted and integrated. Christ represents the light in us. But Christ was crucified between two murderers and we cannot deny them, and certainly not the murderers who live in us.

This is a task for life, but during our adolescence we had a real chance to test our religious sentiment in this respect. The conflict is obvious; the solution is not rebellion nor repression, but integration.

[d] The young adult

Meanwhile, we went to college. What happens in college? College is the period between homes. We have left our parental home and have not yet committed ourselves to a home of our own. We have gone a safe distance from all things Mum and Dad always had to say but we also keep a safe distance from those who want to take away this wonderful vacation from home life. We don't have to worry any more about how to find a compromise between our own ideas and feelings and those of our parents, but on the other hand, we are not yet responsible to any one person in particular. We feel that the time of being educated is over but we are not quite ready to start educating others. In short, we live between two homes, and in a certain way this is the period of the greatest freedom of our life.

In college we also develop a new way of thinking. We learn a scientific approach; the key term is: hypothesis; the criterion: probability; and the tool: experimentation. Only on the basis of an experiment are we willing to accept and reject, and only with a sense of relativity do we want to speak about certainty. For our religious development the college years can become the most ideal time to make our religious ideas and values from 'second-hand fittings into first-hand fittings' (Allport). We may develop enough self-acceptance and creative distance to do some responsible experimentation.

During the college years, a new important aspect of a mature religious sentiment can develop: 'I can be sure without being cocksure' (Allport). As we enter college we take with us many religious concepts and ideas which seemed obvious, and which we never questioned. The question is, whether or not we have the courage to put question marks behind many things; if we can allow ourselves to doubt without losing all grounds. Only he who feels safe in this world can take risks, only he who has a basic trust in the value of life is free to ask many questions without feeling threatened. Trust creates the possibility of a religion of search, which makes a commitment possible without certainty. By the basic trust in the meaning of life we are able to live with a hypothesis, without the need of absolute certainty.

The man who never had any religious doubts during his college years probably walked around blindfolded; he who never experimented with his traditional values and ideas was probably more afraid than free; he who never put to a test any of dad's and mum's advice probably never developed a critical mind; and he who never became irritated by the many ambiguities, ambivalences and hypocrisies in his religious milieu probably never was really satisfied with anything either. But he who did, took a risk. The risk of embarrassing not only his parents but also his friends, the risk of feeling alienated from his past and of becoming irritated by everything religious, even the word 'God'. The risk even of the searing loneliness which Jesus Christ suffered when He cried, 'God, my God, why have you forsaken me?'

In college we can often discover, with pain and frustration, that a mature religious man is very close to the agnostic, and often we have difficulty in deciding which name expresses better our state of mind: agnostic or searching believer. Perhaps they are closer than we tend to think.

[e] The adult man

One facet of adulthood which has special significance for our religious attitude is that the mature adult mind is characterized by a unifying philosophy of life. If we could look at our daily life from above, we might wonder what we are so busy for, so excited about, so concerned with. We might ask with Alfie, 'After all, what is it all about?' And, if there is no real answer to this question, the most honest reaction might be: boredom. Many people who no longer see the meaning of their lives, their daily, often utterly dull, activities, feel bored. Boredom is the dullness of life felt all the way to your stomach. It is the lukewarm quality of daily life, which manifests itself in the repetition of the 'I don't care' phrase. Now if we ask ourselves what boredom really means we might say, 'It is the isolation of experience'. That is to say, we have an experience in life which in no way seems to be connected with the past or the future. Every day seems to be just another day, indifferent, colourless and bleak, just like every other day. This is the mentality in which we need 'kicks' – very short, artificially induced upheavals which, for a while, pull us out of our boredom without really giving any meaning to past or future.

Boredom is the disconnected life, filled with thousands of different words, ideas, thoughts and acts which seem like so many pieces of garbage in stagnant waters. Boredom, which so easily leads to depression, often can become a pervasive feeling, a creeping temptation, difficult to shake off. And certainly, if we have finished school and have a family and a job, this feeling of deep boredom might overwhelm us with the question, 'So what?' Now we have everything, and we will be dead, gone and forgotten in a couple of years, perhaps only remembered because of our oddities and idiosyncracies!

It is in this perspective that a mature, religious sentiment fulfills a creative function. Because it has a unifying power, it brings together the many isolated realities of life and casts them into one meaningful whole. The thousand disconnected pieces fall together and show a pattern which we couldn't see before. All the individuals in the card section of the stadium don't seem to make sense to each other, but from a certain distance, and in a certain perspective, they form a very meaningful word. Just so in a unifying perspective, the many facets of life prove to belong together and point in a definite direction. That is what we refer to if we say that a mature religion gives meaning to life, gives direction, reveals a goal and creates a task to be accomplished. It can make us leave job, country and family to dedicate our life to the suffering poor. It can make us bury ourselves in silence, isolation and contemplation in a Trappist monastery.

This new perspective is what we call faith. It does not create new things but it adds a new dimension to the basic realities of life. It brings our fragmented personality into a meaningful whole, unifies our divided self. It is the source of inspiration for a searching mind, the basis for a creative community and a constant incentive for an on-going renewal of life.

So we come to the end of our trip from Magic to Faith. We started folded up in our mother's womb, one with the world in which we lived. We slowly unfolded out of the magical unity into an autonomous existence, in which we discovered that we

were not alone but stood in a constant dialogue with our surroundings; and we ended by bringing together all the varieties
of life in a new unity – not that of Magic but that of Faith.

Intimacy and Sexuality

&

The Challenge to Love

2

Although I am not writing from the Iron Mountain, I would like to consider this chapter as a 'Report on the Possibility and Desirability of Love'. For the question is not, What should I do if I find myself in deep love with another stranger in this world? but rather, Can this love ever be a reality at all? Many are asking themselves if we are doomed to remain strangers to each other. Is there a spark of misunderstanding in every intimate encounter, a painful experience of separateness in every attempt to unite, a fearful resistance in every act of surrender? Is there a fatal component of hate in the centre of everything we call love?

We probably have wondered in our many lonely moments if there is one corner in this competitive, demanding world where it is safe to be relaxed, to expose ourselves to someone else, and to give unconditionally. It might be very small and hidden. But if this corner exists, it calls for a search through the complexities of our human relationships in order to find it.

How do we go about this? Our plan is first to describe carefully and understand the two main forms of existing, the form of power and the form of love, or in other words, the taking form and the forgiving form, and secondly to examine how these forms are related to destruction and to creation. Only then are we ready to ask the crucial question: Is love a utopian dream or a possibility within our reach?

[A] THE TAKING FORM

Our attention goes first to the taking form of existence, which is the form of power. Let me start by introducing the man who suffers from a constant fear that everything is too much for him. Everything, I mean. It just seems that he is no longer able to keep the many pieces of his life together in a meaningful unity. He is nervous and trembling, tense and restless, and he has lost his usual ability to concentrate and create. He says, 'I can't function any longer. Everybody likes me, my friends think a lot of me – but they don't really know me. If they found out who I really am and how I really feel, they wouldn't want to look at me any longer. I know that I often hate instead of love, that I sometimes want to hurt instead of cure, to kill instead of heal. You know, I am a hypocrite.' Few people will say this. Perhaps we sometimes say it to ourselves and find ourselves caught in a prison of fear. 'If they really knew us, they would stop loving us.' It is the fear of being trapped, of being taken.

Let us have a closer look at this all-pervasive taking form.[1] When you take a teacup by its handle, you can keep it at a distance and look at it from all sides. You can make it an obedient instrument in your hands. You can manipulate it in any direction you want. You have complete control over it, for it is in your hands, your power. Many of our human relationships are of this order. When you are mad at a four-year-old and take him by his ear and shake his head like a teacup, he feels offended, humiliated, treated like an object. When at a party, you take a freshman by his nose, pull his leg, or pinch his cheeks, he feels taken. But worse than these physical forms is the mental form in which we can take our fellow man. We can take him by his vulnerable

[1] Cf., Ludwig Binswanger, *Grundformen und Erkenntnis Menschlichen Daseins* (Max Niehans Verlag Zürich: 1953), pp. 266-281.

spot, his hidden weakness, and make him an object at which we can look from a distance, which we can turn around and lead to the place we want it to go. You see how this form of taking is a form of power. It has the structure of blackmailing, in which we keep the other's weakness behind our back, until the moment we can use it against him at the time he blocks our way.

There are too many illustrations in our life to deny the dominating role of this taking form of existence. When you sit together and talk in a free and relaxed fashion about a friend you like very much, it might happen that a stranger walks in and says: 'Who are you talking about? About Mary? Oh, that sexpot ...' You freeze. Mary has become an object, a thing, a piece of conversation, and the dialogue dies and often is perverted into a verbal combat. When a psychologist revels in discovering that his patient is a classic example of an obsessive neurotic and sends him home with the new label, gratified by his good diagnosis, he takes him by his weakness and substitutes classification for cure. When people go through your life history to check your past and find your weak spot which can be used against you, should you move in a direction opposite to their power, they operate in the taking form. The Russian author, Daniel, one of the victims of a recent writers' trial, describes in vivid terms how the revelation of a dark spot in someone's past can drive him into isolation, despair and finally total disintegration. Knowing someone's past can be the most lethal weapon in human relationships, which can bring about shame, guilt, moral and even physical death.

But we don't need such dramatic examples. Is not every student, who fills out application forms for graduate schools, and every professor, who writes letters of recommendation, obedient to the taking structure of our life? We are judged, evaluated, tested, and graded, diagnosed and classified from the time our parents compared our first walk with a little neighbour's.

Gradually, as time goes on, we realize that our permanent record is building its own life, independent of ours. It is really not so amazing that we often feel caught, taken, and used for purposes not our own. The main concern then becomes not who I am but who I am considered to be, not what I think, but what others think of me.

In this taking existence we find ourselves operating in terms of power, motivated by fear. We are armed to our teeth, carefully following the movements of the other, waiting to hit back at the right moment and in the vulnerable spot. If we don't, we just might miss the right job, the good grad school, the assignment in Alaska (which we had hoped for during the Vietnam crisis), or even the man or woman we hoped to marry. And so, often in very subtle forms we envelop ourselves in the cocoon of our taking world.

Even understanding people, which seems the opposite of taking them, becomes stained by power. 'Psychological under-standing' then means having an idea about the hidden motives of people. It is like saying: 'You don't have to tell me. I know that fellow.' Hours of therapy and counselling can be wasted by the client trying to figure out what technique the counsellor uses. Isn't this true also for many dating relationships? Sometimes it seems that a boy feels more relaxed in the classroom than when he is alone with a girl. Instead of feeling free to give his affection, express freely his moods and concerns to the girl he loves, he is more self-conscious than ever, wants to make the right remark at the right time, and is everything but spontaneous. What looks from a distance like love is often, at a closer look, fear. I am saying, 'I don't want to become a pawn, to be pushed around. I want to keep control over the situation. And after all – it is always better to drop than to be dropped.'

All this leaves us with the suspicion that the reality which we call 'love' is nothing other than a blanket to cover the real fact that a man and a woman conquer each other in a long, subtle skirmish of taking movements in which one is always the winner who manipulates the other in the patterns of his or her life. Love seems to be unmasked as another taking of our fellow man and exercising of our subtle but pervasive power over him.

If this is true, destruction becomes an inescapable aspect of our existence, for the taking form of life means that our weakness can always be held against us and that there is no place in life where we are safe. Thomas Merton in his study about nonviolence has shown how this taking mode of existence is based on the concept of the irreversibility of evil. Your mistakes, failures, and offences are unchangeable elements on the record of your life. Evil then is definitive and unchangeable. The only solution for the irreversible is its destruction. If evil cannot be reversed and forgiven, the only thing those living the taking mode can do with it is to cut it out, to uproot it, to burn it to ashes. In its full consequences this means that tenderness, sympathy, and love can only be considered as weaknesses to be eliminated, and that every mistake is final and unforgiveable. Then a misplaced gesture becomes a haunting memory, a bitter word creates an excruciating remorse, and a faithless moment leads to despair and destruction of life.

These are the dynamics of war and hate. If we look at the thousands of people suffering in mental institutions, the millions of children crushed in the conflict between their parents, the endless number of people separated from each other and left alone, we wonder if anybody can ever escape the taking form of our existence. It is the form of power which brings destruction unless the power is ours.

In this perspective, imprisoned in the vicious circle of taking, power and final destruction, we find ourselves doomed to the impossibility of love. Not without sarcasm in his voice, the man of power will say: 'Love, peace and forgiveness are the dreams of those who have not yet entered the vicious circle. But wait until the day when their most primitive impulse to survive will speak its irresistible language. Then they will not only take life, they will grab it.'

[B] THE FORGIVING FORM, WHICH IS THE FORM OF LOVE

But the man who dared to trust us said: 'If my friends found out who I really am and how I really feel, they would not look at me any longer, they would spit on me and leave me alone with my hypocrisy.' This man has drastically broken through the closed circle. Somehow he has jumped far beyond the reasonable and has broken through the walls of shame. He has believed that confession is a possibility. When a man cries, when the walls of his self-composure break down and he is able to express his deepest despair, weakness, hate and jealousy, his meanness and inner division, he somewhere believes that we will not take and destroy him. As if a voice told him: 'Don't be afraid to tell.'

Maybe we remember the few occasions in our life in which we were able to show someone we love our real self: not only our great successes but also our weaknesses and pains, not only our good intentions but also our bitter motives, not only our radiant face but also our dark shadow. It takes a lot of courage, but it might just open a new horizon, a new way of living. It is this breaking through the closed circle, often described as a conversion experience, which may come suddenly and unexpectedly or slowly and gradually. People might call us a crazy idealist, an unrealistic dreamer, a first class romanticist, but it does not touch us very deeply because we know with a new form of certainty which we had never experienced before that peace, forgiveness, justice, and inner freedom are more than mere words. Conversion is the discovery of the possibility of love.

How can we understand this loving form of existence in which the taking form is transcended? Love is not based on the willingness to listen, to understand problems of others, or to tolerate their otherness. Love is based on the mutuality of the confession of our total self to each other. This makes us free to declare not only: 'My strength is your strength' but also: 'Your pain is my pain, your weakness is my weakness, your sin is my sin.' It is in this intimate fellowship of the weak that love is born. When the exposure of one's deepest dependency becomes an invitation to share this most existential experience, we enter a new area of life. For in this sharing of weakness violence can be overcome. When we are ready to throw stones – words can be as sharp as stones – someone just may have the courage to cry out: 'He who is without sin, let him throw the first stone.'

If we are willing to believe that the wheat can only come to full maturity if we allow the weeds to exist in the same field, we don't have to be afraid of every conflict and avoid every argument. It is here where love creates a smile, and where humour can be soft instead of cynical. You know the situation. John and Sally walk in the park. After a ten minute exposition by John about Hegel, Kierkegaard, Camus, Sartre and some other of his recent authors, there is a long silence. Sally asks, 'John, do you care for me?' John becomes a little irritated, 'Of course I do, but I wanted to know what you think about existentialism.' Sally: 'John I don't want to marry a philosopher. I want to marry you.' John becomes mad. 'Don't be so silly and stupid, if we can't have a decent conversation, how can we ever get along?' Sally: 'There is a little more to love than a decent conversation, and I just don't want to be another of your classmates.'

Well, they had a short walk that evening. But perhaps later they could laugh about it and say, 'At least we were not afraid to show our real feelings.' If John and Sally would have been only sweet, understanding and agreeing with each other they might have doubted if they really were free to love. And it is exactly there, where love becomes visible.

Let us examine some characteristics of love. Love first of all is *truthful*. In the fellowship of the weak the truth creates the unshakable base on which we feel free to move. Truth means primarily the full acceptance of our basic human condition, which says that no man has power over any other man. Faithfulness is only possible if constantly guided by the truth of the human situation which prevents us from fictitiousness, shallowness, and simulation.

The second characteristic of love is its *tenderness*. Perhaps nowhere does it become so clear that love transcends the taking form than in its tenderness. In love hands don't take, grasp or hold. They caress. Caressing is the possibility of human hands to be tender. The careful touch of the hand makes for growth. Like a gardener who carefully touches the flowers to enable the light to shine through and stimulate growth, the hand of the lover allows for the full self-expression of the other. In love the mouth does not bite, devour or destroy. It kisses. A kiss is not to take in, but to allow for the full and fearless surrender. In love the eyes don't trap the stranger's body through a Sartrian keyhole, nor do they arouse shame by the feeling of being exposed as Noah felt when his son Ham looked at his naked body; but in love the eyes cover the other's body with the warm radiation of an admiring smile as an expression of tenderness.

Finally and most importantly, love asks for a total *disarmament*. The encounter in love is an encounter without weapons. Perhaps the disarmament in the individual encounter is more difficult than international disarmament. We are very able to hide our guns and knives even in the most intimate relationship. An old bitter memory, a slight suspicion about motives, or a small doubt can be as sharp as a knife held behind our back as a weapon for defence in case of attack. Can we ever meet a fellow man without any protection? Reveal ourselves to him in our total vulnerability? This is the heart of our question. Are man and woman able to exclude the power in their relationship and become totally available for each other? When the soldier sits down to eat he lays down his weapons, because eating means peace and rest. When he stretches out his body to sleep he is more vulnerable than ever. Table and bed are the two places of intimacy where love can manifest itself in weakness. In love men and women take off all the forms of power, embracing each other in total disarmament. The nakedness of their body is only a symbol of total vulnerability and availability.

When the physical encounter of men and women in the intimate act of intercourse is not an expression of their total availability to each other, the creative fellowship of the weak is not yet reached. Every sexual relationship with built-in reservations, with mental restrictions or time limits, is still part of the taking structure. It means 'I want you now, but not tomorrow. I want something from you, but I don't want *you*.' Love is limitless. Only when men and women give themselves to each other in total surrender, that is, with their whole person for their whole life, can their encounter bear full fruits. When through the careful growth of their relationship men and women have come to the freedom of total disarmament, their giving also becomes for-giving, their nakedness does not evoke shame but desire to share, and their ultimate vulnerability becomes the core of their mutual strength. New life is born in the state of total vulnerability – this is the mystery of love. Power kills. Weakness creates. It creates autonomy, self-awareness and freedom. It creates openness to give and receive in mutuality. And finally it creates the good ground on which new life can come to full development and maturity. This explains why the highest safeguard for the physical, mental and spiritual health of the child is not primarily the attention paid to the child but the unrestricted love of the parents for each other.

If the taking form of existence were the only possibility, destruction would be our fate. But if love can be found, creation can exist. Because love is based, as Merton says, on the belief in the reversibility of evil. Evil then is not final and unchangeable. Gandhi's concept of nonviolence was essentially based on his conviction that forgiveness could change every enemy into a friend, that in hatred love is hidden, in despair hope, in doubt faith, in evil good, in sin redemption. Love is an act of forgiving in which evil is converted to good and destruction into creation. In the truthful, tender, and disarmed encounter of love man is able to create. In this perspective it becomes clear that the sexual act is a religious act. Out of the total disarmament of man on his cross, exposing himself in his extreme vulnerability, the new man arises and manifests himself in freedom. Is it not exactly in this same act of self-surrender that we find our highest fulfilment which expresses itself in the new life we create? Religion and sexuality, which in the past have been so often described as opponents, merge into one and the same reality when they are seen as an expression of the total self-surrender in love.

[C] THE POSSIBILITY OF LOVE

Having described the taking form and the loving form, the form which can destroy by power and the form which can create through forgiving, we have to return to our original question: 'Is love a utopian dream or a possibility within our reach?' Let us start here by saying that our life is often a very painful fluctuation between the two desires to take and to forgive. We want to be ambitious and competitive but sometimes we want to forgive.

We want strength and successes, but sometimes we feel a desire to confess our other side. We want to kill, but also to cure, to hurt but also to help. Although the world in which we live keeps suggesting that realism is an outlook on life based on power, confusing but at the same time attractive prophets keep saying that there is another possible alternative, the alternative of love. They all seem to ask for conversion, change of mind. But we don't know if we really can take the risk.

And we have good reasons to be afraid. Love means openness, vulnerability, availability and confession. When our friend says, 'If my friends found out how I really feel, if I would show my real self, then they would no longer love me but hate me' – he speaks about a real possibility. It is very risky to be honest, because someone just might not respond with love, but take us by our weak spot and turn it against ourselves. Our confession might destroy us. Revealing our past failures and present ambivalences can make us losers. We can be thrown away in a gesture of contempt. This is not only a possibility but a cruel fact in the lives of many who feel that love and forgiveness is a utopian fantasy of flower children.

It is obvious that the taking structure is so much a part of our existence that we cannot avoid it. Don't ask the telephone operator how she is feeling today. Don't start a conversation about the prayer life of the man from whom you want to buy some stamps at the post office. Don't ask your teacher about his sexual behaviour. You destroy human communication because you want to play a game without rules, which means no game at all. We are wise enough to prefer in most situations the taking form. Wise as the oyster who keeps his hard shell tightly closed to protect his tender and vulnerable self. Our problem therefore is not how we can completely annihilate the taking structure of life but whether there is any possibility at all to transcend that structure, to open our shell even when it is only somewhat, somewhere, somehow, sometime.

How often is the intimate encounter of two persons an expression of their total freedom? Many people are driven into each other's arms in fear and trembling. They embrace each other in despair and loneliness. They cling to each other to prevent worse things from happening. Their sleep together is only an expression of their desire to escape the threatening world, to forget their deep frustration, to ease for a minute the unbearable tension of a demanding society, to experience some warmth, protection, and safety. Their privacy does not create a place where they both can grow in freedom and share their mutual discoveries, but a fragile shelter in a storming world.

But can it be anything else, we wonder, if the only real and final solution to life is death. If we don't know where we come from or where we are going, if life is a trembling little flame between two darknesses, if we are thrown into this existence only to be swallowed by it, then being secure seems more pathological than real. In that case there is nothing else left for us to do but to try to survive and use all possible power to keep the flame burning. Is this cowardice? Perhaps. But it often seems better to be a coward than to be dead.

Here the psychologist stops and the philosopher finishes his last sentences with a question mark. Here we also should stop – unless someone is able to cut through the vicious circle. Indeed, it seems that sometimes in the depths of our despair and in the loneliness of our prison, we do not become hardened and bitter but open and sensitive for the voice of a new man. Those who want to hear him can hear him and those who want to read him can read him. To many he is a source of irritation and anger, for a few a sign of hope. In ecstasy the new man proclaims:

> Something which has existed since the beginning, that we
> have heard and have seen with our own eyes; that we have
> watched and touched with our hands: ... this is our subject ...
> God is light, there is no darkness in him at all ... If we live our
> lives in the light, as he is in the light, we are in union with one
> another ... (1 John 1:17).

Suddenly everything is converted into its opposite. Darkness
into light, enslavement into freedom, death into life, taking into
giving, destruction into creation and hate into love. With an irresistible strength the voice breaks through the vicious circle of
our existence saying:

> Let us love one another since love comes from God ... (1 John
> 4:7). In love there can be no fear, but fear is driven out by per-
> fect love: because to fear is to expect punishment, and anyone
> who is afraid is still imperfect in love (1 John 4:18). (But)
> God is greater than our heart (1 John 3:20). We have to love,
> because he loved us first (1 John 4:19).

What else does this mean besides the redeeming revelation that
love *is* a possibility? Perhaps the best definition of revelation is
the uncovering of the truth that it is safe to love. The walls of our
anxiety, our anguish, our narrowness are broken down and a
wide endless horizon is shown. 'We have to love, because he
loved us first.' It is safe to embrace in vulnerability because we
both find ourselves in loving hands. It is safe to be available
because someone told us that we stand on solid ground. It is
safe to surrender because we will not fall into a dark pit but
enter a welcoming home. It is safe to be weak because we are
surrounded by a creative strength.

To say and live this is a new way of knowing. We are not
surrounded by darkness but by light. He who knows this light

will see it. The cripple will walk, the deaf hear, the mute speak, the blind see, and the mountains move. Someone has appeared to us and said: The sign of love is the sign of weakness: A baby wrapped in swaddling clothes and lying in a manger. That is the glory of God, the peace of the world and the good will of all men.

I could not find any other language than this to express that love has become a possibility. If there is a need for a new morality it is the morality which teaches us the fellowship of the weak as a human possibility. Love then is not a clinging to each other in the fear of an oncoming disaster but an encounter in a freedom that allows for the creation of new life. This love cannot be proved. We can only be invited to it and find it to be true by an engaging response. As long as we experience the Christian life as a life which puts restrictions on our freedom of expression, we have perverted and inverted its essence. The core message of Christianity is exactly this message of the possibility of transcending the taking form of our human existence. The main witness of this message is Jesus who in the exposure of His total vulnerability broke through the chains of death and found His life by losing it. He challenges us to break through the circle of our imprisonment. He challenges us to face our fellow man without fear and to enter with Him in the fellowship of the weak, knowing that it will not bring destruction but creation, new energy, new life, and – in the end – a new world.

Intimacy and Prayer

෨

3

Student-Prayers: Between Confusion and Hope

When we ask about the prayerlife of today's college student we ask to enter into a very intimate world. It is the world where the student faces the ultimate meaning of his existence and tries to relate to what stretches beyond the limits of his birth and death. Entering this world can only happen on invitation. Every form of force will harm this most sensitive area of life and even ruin the same realities which we want to understand.

But why enter at all? Shouldn't this most private domain remain private at all cost? Yet what sounds like respect and protection of a man's individuality might in fact be a fearful avoidance to experience the deepest possible level of human communication. A man who wants to share his prayer wants to share his life, and not just as a sequence of events, emotions and thoughts. He wants to share a moment in which the question of the meaning of existence can be raised. And perhaps it is exactly in the sharing of his prayer that a man is able to reveal his God to his fellow man.

Based on this conviction, some university students asked their friends to write a prayer. There was no sampling involved, no systematic selection, no careful divisions into groups, college years or family background. The most simple question was asked: 'Are you willing to write a prayer?' The response to this question was the first discovery: 'Yes. Yes, I would like to try.

Nobody asked me before, but I would like to write a prayer and I will ask my friends too.' Friends asked friends and within two months a collection grew of 41 prayers written by students of both sexes, with a wide variety of attitudes and views on life. Some students were used to praying, others never prayed. Some lived with an easy familiarity in the house of God, others wondered if the word 'God' made any sense at all. Some took life as a happy selection of good things, others as a torture chamber with closed windows. Some were regular churchgoers, others never went or had stopped going because of boredom or unbelief. But all wrote a prayer and wanted others to read it. And while the collection went from hand to hand, evoking many different reactions, students found themselves reading a prayer-book, which is a rather exceptional kind of book to read on today's college campus.

In this study I would like to present these prayers, not to draw any general conclusion about the religious life of the students, but simply as one of the many witnesses of man's ongoing search for meaning. One of the students who read all the prayers with great care and sensitivity wrote: 'A personal prayer falls always, I think, between disciplines or definitions. Something lurks behind the words too personal, too elusive to get at with any system of rigorous analysis. Despite this difficulty a reader can understand and describe what is going on in a particular prayer, and with maturity, sensitivity and attention he may come to understand much of that which lies beneath the words and phrases strung together to make up that prayer.'[1] With this same attitude I hope to be able to describe the world of prayer as visible through this collection.

But is there any perspective within which we can place this wide variety of individual expressions? After studying the

[1] R. Bradley.

prayers it seemed that they touched two extreme experiences: the experience of total confusion and self-doubt in which the student finds himself asking for clarity and self-understanding and the experience of a strong and definitive hope, characterized by self-awareness, self-acceptance and the expectance of greater things to come. We find the praying student somewhere between these poles of confusion and hope. So also can we locate in a tentative way the divergent prayers. Taking them together we even can see a movement out of the prison of self-doubt to the freedom of self-confirmation. And moving between these two poles we encounter many Gods, with many faces and many tasks. Most visible in this collection are the following Gods:

1 'The clarifying God'
2 'The banned God'
3 'The big buddy God'
4 'The compassionate God'
5 'The beautiful God'
6 'The giving God'
7 'The coming God'

I. THE CLARIFYING GOD

Under the mask of a self-assertive attitude many students hide deep feelings of confusion. Bombarded by millions of contradicting stimuli, confronted with opposing viewpoints, ideals and desires, they often feel lost in the stream of events and feelings and wonder who they are and where they are going. Many are persecuted by the question: 'Can I do anything meaningful in this mad world, which speaks one day about nonviolence and the other day about revolution, one day about a crusade in

Europe and the other day about murder in Vietnam?' In the middle of all this confusion they have lost track of their ideas, feelings and emotions and have become entangled in the complexity of their internal life.

When these students pray they are confronted with their own confusion. 'What can I do?' or 'What do I want?' is a question, but a more basic question is 'What do I feel?' And this confusion of mind and cluttering of feelings can lead to an inability to experience the many differentiations in life. Joy and sadness, anger and thankfulness, love and hate seem to blend into a paralyzing lump of unidentifiable emotions. The result is often apathy, dullness, fatigue. Overstimulated, overexposed, overfed with ideals and slogans stretched in too many different directions, nothing else can be said than: 'I don't care.' A dull passivity has become the only possible attitude. While students are preparing themselves for a great Mardi Gras, one of them prays:

> Well, here we are, another Mardi-Gras weekend – for some a time of fun, enjoyment, thoughtfulness and forgetfulness, and for some a time of depression and anger.
>
> But for me neither: and that just about sums up the whole apathetic slump. It is serious and has got to the point where its causes – the library, the war, the ugliness, the jokes, the intolerance – have broken most enthusiasm to the point where drifting is the only thing possible.
>
> I don't think that I like drifting – oh, not a rat race, just some enthusiasm, some interest, and then I can at least pursue something, even though that something may be shaded.
>
> Please help everyone to find enthusiasm and interest.

Out of his dullness and apathy this student asks for articulation and differentiation to find some new handles and directions in the labyrinth of the inner life and rediscover himself within some clear boundaries of identifiable experiences.

This confusion often leads to a very negative self-evaluation. Many students experience vaguely self-contempt, even self-hate. They have lost self-respect and are angry with their own unknown self. You cannot love what you do not know and how can you love yourself, when the only thing you experience is a deep pit of intermingled impulses, feelings, emotions and ideas, of which you are more victim than master? Out of this confusion one student prays:

> Help me find and cherish myself – to solve the problems of myself and others, to more clearly see the direction in which I'm going. It has been so cloudy and jerky – sometimes I wonder if I'm progressing at all – and sometimes I wonder if I can. Remove this doubt I have about myself – or better let me see the doubt and lack of confidence for what it is, and in removing it, learn more of it. I can see in my actions how my doubt and lack of confidence come out. I hide it well, but hiding it makes me worry all the more. Help me remove this self-consciousness which makes me second-guess myself. Let me cease to try to impose a definition on myself, but to act and think naturally. Let me see that all are to be respected, many are to be loved, some must be fought – and that all men are more than I think they are.

And even praying itself becomes nearly an impossibility. There is so little distance and so much cloudiness that praying creates guilt and enters in the vicious circle of a growing self-devaluation.

> Lord, I don't really feel like praying. I'm confused, everything is confused. I don't know what I'll be doing next year – I don't even know for sure what I want to be doing next year, or

what I should be doing. I feel guilty praying – turning to you at a time like this because I feel two-faced to pray only when I need help and not to pray when I don't.

But somewhere there is a spark of light, hardly noticeable and very subtle. The attitude of praying can sometimes create that little bit of distance which is the beginning of self-knowledge. Praying, if it is anything more than a narcissistic self-complaint, involves someone else, another who is not just me. And in this way we can see that the expression of confusion can become the beginning of its solution. Praying then means creating distance and God's answer is given in the praying act. One student after a long prayer filled with spiritual dizziness and self-doubt writes this short postscriptum:

This must be a prayer, because it has done something already. As you think about things, they become clearer, and kind of fall into place. I don't think that thinking about problems ever solves any alone, but at least gives a basis for further action and further thought.

Here the clarifying God reveals Himself. Here the first step is set out of confusion. Here a road becomes visible and man can at least start to walk on his own feet. New channels of energy become available and the result of this prayer is that a man can feel that he can do something himself. The student's post-script is a beautiful echo of Anton Boisen's conviction: 'I do believe in prayer. I believe that its chief function is – to find out what is wanted of us and to enable us to draw upon sources of strength which will make it possible for us to accomplish our task whatever it may be.'[2]

[2] Anton Boisen, *Out of the Depth* (Harper & Brothers: 1960), p. 111.

Prayer opens our eyes for ourselves and through clarification enables us to step forward in the direction of hope.

2. THE BANNED GOD

Sometimes the step out of confusion means a step away from God. It is not seldom that man found internal rest and harmony once he had the courage to shake off his torturing God. His present Godless life feels like a liberation after years of painful and humiliating occupation. This experience of change is a conversion experience in reverse, but with the same psychological effects: new internal freedom, growing self-respect, new hope. For some students their God-ridden past is filled with memories of scrupulosity, guilt-feelings, fear for punishment, unbearable responsibilities and unlivable expectations. They felt surrounded by a wall of prohibitions and deprived by God's cruel omnipotence, omniscience and omnipresence from their own self-respect. Exposed in their miserable nakedness to God's intruding eye they were like men robbed of their most intimate identity. For these individuals the murder of their God was an experience of conversion, and the way to self-discovery, self-respect, self-awareness and self-affirmation. They had to have the courage to ban their tyrannical God and to claim back their own most personal individuality.

Therefore, prayer to a nonexisting God, the banned God, is not an embarrassing joke, but a deep and sincere expression of a paradise gained. Such a prayer can show how thin the edge is between agnosticism and Christian faith. The banning of God has created a new peace of mind and a fearless heart. One student prays:

When I speak to you I strongly suspect that You aren't 'out there' now and never were. I have lost You and I feel better for it because You diminished me and wouldn't let me be myself. I always felt I had to consider what You wanted me to do, what image or state of perfection You demanded.

Since the time of our separation I've grown more selfish. I'm concerned a lot with myself, with my own development as a human being. I suppose I still want to be perfect, but not for my own sake, nor to please You. What matters now are the others.

This is a real prayer. What makes it a prayer? It is a dialogue, a conversation. That means that here one is not rigid, closed, bitter and cynical, but open to a response, willing to listen and available for growth. It is the same student who prays:

If and when I find You again – and I'm certainly leaving myself open to that – I just know that I'll find You in the others and in my Self. Who knows, maybe You are what is best in each of us.

God has become an obstacle in man's desire to be good for his neighbour. Instead of the way to the other, He is in the way. A prayer to such a God becomes an act of cowardice or just weakness. A student painfully aware of the contradiction involved in his praying attitudes describes his conversion from God to men as follows:

There just doesn't seem to be any real reason to pray – I don't say prayers any more. I'm still not really convinced that there is such a thing as a God. You don't achieve or receive anything aside from your own ambitions and work or from another. Thanking people involved in a specific situation seems much more relevant than thanking God.

There is someone more important than God, that is man. God-talk is boring, trivial, fruitless and vicious. It keeps us away from what really matters. With a new found freedom a student says:

> I can't be bothered with the trivial things the church worries about. It just seems a waste of time.

In all these prayers, or nonprayers, God is experienced as blocking the way to the self and therefore to the other. The prayer for self-discovery is a prayer asking God to leave, sometimes forcing Him to get out of the way in order to find freedom and self. So a man steps out of his confusion by banning a suffocating God from his existence.

3. THE BIG-BUDDY-GOD

In a seemingly drastic contrast with the banned God, we encounter in the student-prayers the big-buddy-God. It is the God with whom you can talk with an easy-going familiarity. In a remarkable way God combines the qualities of a playmate and a cure all. He is like a big brother, part of the family, but stronger and willing to solve with a friendly smile the worries of the baby boy. You can speak to Him in a shoulder slapping way and brag about Him when you need some support in your self-esteem. You can count on Him every moment and you can forget about your own problems, since He is around all the time, never too tired to help out. One prayer to this big-buddy-God reads as follows:

> Lord, there are an awful lot of things that bug me lately. The real uncertainty of next year, especially all the people I snub every day – as a result of a lot of stagnant relationships. Really, Lord, I'm a pretty imperfect specimen – basically, Lord, help

me to keep trying to love a little bit better and to be a little bit more open to others. Also, Lord, help me to become what You want me to become. Help me to choose the right law school, the right wife, and the right job – make money insignificant – Also remember the guys at home, the guys at school, those getting married and those in Vietnam.

So Lord, I'm going to play handball now, and I'd like to ask just one more thing of You, that is, help me to live more vibrantly what I believe or at least what I think I believe. Help me to take serious every event in life especially every person, and understand it or him, not condemn it or him. Okay?

P.S. Thanks for dying on the cross for me and my friends.

The casual tone of this prayer is like that of a boy comfortably sitting on daddy's lap. There are many problems, but they don't cut deep, they don't really hurt. They hardly touch the heart of the praying man. If there is confusion, it is confusion of an external nature, which doesn't cause internal turmoil but which can be dealt with by a direct request for help with the unshakable conviction that everything will be okay soon.

This attitude comes close to what William James calls the once-born, healthy-minded type of religion. It is the religion of the man 'who's soul is of this sky-blue sort, whose affinities are rather with flowers and birds and all enchanting innocencies than with dark human passions, who can think no ill of man or God, and in whom religious gladness, being in possession from the outset, needs no deliverance from any antecedent burden.'[3] William James does not hide his suspicion about this 'ultra-optimistic form of the once-born philosophy'.[4] He points up the

---

[3] William James, *The Varieties of Religious Experience* (Enlarged edition. University Books: 1963), p. 80.
[4] *ibid.*, 362.

superficial nature of a religion in which all evil is externalized and not recognized as a part of man asking for conversion. This superficiality of the once-born-minded is also obvious in this prayer:

> Hey, Big Man. Things are in a sorry state right now. The whole country is in an uproar. You know, I never really thought about it much. I mean in terms of affecting me. Martin Luther King was kind of off in the distance. He was a rabble-rouser. He confronted the people with something new, different and unpleasant. It made me stop and think. I don't have any conclusions though. I don't imagine You like this mess we've gotten ourselves in, but help us out of it, please?

Remarkable here is that the student himself is more or less aware of his own uninvolvement and aloof distance. But although he recognizes vaguely his lack of personal responsibility he still expects the solution to come from his big-buddy-Jesus.

If we analyse both prayers more closely we see that we can hardly discover any real hope. These prayers are still on the level of wish-fulfilment. Wishes are concrete; 'They have specific objects and articulate contents.'[5] The wish wants something very specific and belongs more to the surprise level of Santa Claus than to the personalistic level of faith.

The big-buddy prayers which we quoted are filled with wishes and expect God to surprise man soon with His great divine gift. These prayers therefore, are still far away from self-knowledge, self-acceptance and hope. Although they seem so opposite from the prayers to the banned God, they are very close to them when

---

[5] See Paul Pruyser, 'Phenomenology and Dynamics of Hoping,' *Journal for the Scientific Study of Religion* 3:86–96 (Fall 1963) and, *A Dynamic Psychology of Religion* (Harper & Row: 1968), pp. 166–170.

we see them on the continuum from confusion to hope. This kind of prayer is free from confusion, but not by facing the problems, but by banning them or not allowing them to enter into the inner life. The internal rest of the man who has shaken off the bothersome God is just as superficial as the relaxed attitude of him who talks to God as a divine playmate.

4. THE COMPASSIONATE GOD

In the long row of prayers there is a turning point where a new perspective is breaking through. No entangling confusion nor easy rest, but the beginning of something different pointing to hope, vaguely, hesitantly and tentatively, but clearly recognizably. These prayers can best be called anti-heroic prayers. They ask for a creative passivity in a demanding, competitive world.

They are the crying out of a man who uses grades as a measure for success, success as a basis of promotion and promotion as a criterion of human value. They also are a protest against the desires to become a star, to be worshipped for exceptional results, or honoured for bravery. They are prayers to a compassionate God, who does not ask for heroic martyrdom, but wants to embrace a weak man.

> Father, I ask not that you give me strength nor bravery, nor humility, nor courage. These are but words, straining futilely to compress and to define that which was meant to be open. The more I grasp for these man-made ideas, the more I fail. In the end all words, all exhortations seem little more than hollow clatter. When I listen to these words my life becomes a task, a challenge – and always I fail. Such thinking urges me to 'try a little harder'. And I fail again. And so on in an endless circular parade both led and followed by proud men.

Perhaps this frustration is your silent voice begging me to stop, to let you carry my 'burden'. Whenever I do stop, there is no burden. Then I sense your presence in the stillness, a stillness flowing far beneath the sterile incongruency of man alone.

I should ask for nothing, just wait for you to give. But I am impatient and must ask. Father, help me to receive the peace which you constantly offer; help me to hear the frozen stillness of your harmony; help me to be passive; help me to accept; help me to stop.

This sounds like a prayer of an exhausted circus dancer who feels that he can lose balance at any moment and fall from the thin rope in the middle of a roaring crowd. It is the voice of a tired man, tired from the unceasing request to do better, to try harder, to climb higher. It is the cry of a man doubting if he will be able to keep pace with the fast-moving world, and fearful of falling apart under the growing burden of his demanding milieu.

This praying man wants to stop, to surrender in the soft caressing hands of an understanding God, to fall asleep in safe arms, to cry without fear, to let go, relax his tense muscles and rest long and deep, forgetting the cold, cruel and hostile world. In many ways this prayer represents an anticlimax to the banner-waving type of Christianity, in which the brave heroic youth willing to give his life for his commanding God was extolled as an example for all lukewarm believers. It is the other side of the man stimulated and challenged from many pulpits to fight his way through this dangerous world and secure through utmost efforts everlasting rewards in the future-life.

But perhaps we are shortsighted when we only see here a reaction to a triumphalistic past. Perhaps we find here the nucleus of the new mystic, the beginning of a prayer which is not the result of human concentration, but of the emptiness created for the divine Spirit. We can catch a glimpse of this new mysticism when we recognize the new sense of humility shining through the antiheroic prayer. They are smiling prayers, in which man asks for a little bit of happiness, a little bit of beauty, a little bit of meaning in life. One student prays:

> I don't want to live in vain – Make me live for something – I'm no hero. I don't really have whatever it is that makes a hero. But I don't want to be a coward. I don't want to be afraid when the time for courage arrives. Let me do something. Let me do it in my own quiet unheroic way. If I can just be remembered as being a good man, as being a distinct and different man, I will feel that I did not waste my life. If I feel that my living here, that the very fact that I existed and lived on earth, meant something to someone, I will be happy. Let me be remembered by someone. Let me help someone – Don't permit me to just exist as another human being. Make me live. I don't want to live in vain.

The beauty is modesty. The fatigue is less obvious here. The humble desire to be of some good to someone is central. But there very well might have been a purifying experience which made this prayer possible. There is a new rest and freedom not the result of repression or avoidance, but based on the humble recognition of man's important but small place in the face of his Creator.

5. THE BEAUTIFUL GOD

On our way out of confusion we have passed the point where something new was breaking through. In the prayers to the compassionate God we discovered a new openness, a new receptivity which gave room to a creative relationship to the 'reality of the unseen' (William James). And although there was still much reaction against the spy-God, the cry for compassion and understanding also meant an opening of the senses for new experiences.

We now come to a group of prayers which can be seen as a dramatic plea for sensitivity. In these prayers students ask to be in touch with what is real, to experience in depth the world which surrounds us and to feel united with the vital sources of life. They look for oneness and a liberation from the painful sense of alienation. They want to touch, taste, smell, hear and see what is beyond their own loneliness and surrender to the unspeakable beauty of the divine. They are prayers to the beautiful God, beautiful in a sensual way, in which the analytical distance is broken down in an ecstatic joy making God into a bodily experience. The alienation out of which these prayers are born is most dramatically verbalized by the student who writes:

> Alone while in class
> Alone with my friends
> Alone in a pressing crowd
> Where to turn to shelter this all embracing shell?
>
> The world is without life – no longer a friend
> The trees sticky leaves, children;
> All seem – only unreal.
> They out there. I am apart.

Out of this isolation the impulse to dive back into the womb of existence speaks its urging language. These prayers are like prayers of the American Indians who aspired not to be master over the world or to rule creation in God's name but only to merge with nature and experience the participation with the creative forces of life. In their masks the face of man merges with the body of a lizard or snake and in their rituals they hoped to reach the sense of their brotherly place in nature.

This same desire is visible in some of the students who let their hair grow free, dress in a loose unrestrained way, speak about beautiful things and beautiful people and eat the seeds which help them enter in the passive state where colours and sounds embrace them with a tender touch. Central is the desire to step away from the meagre emotions of a technocratic society in which superficiality leads to boredom and the breaking of contact with the mysterious powers of reality. And this brings us to a new prayer:

> Help us to see that which is real. A reality. Help us to lie under a tree and enjoy the grass and sky and wind, to have a definitive feeling, perhaps simple, perhaps deep, to think wildly, openly to stretch.
>
> To hold a hand and mean it, to appreciate beauty, to experience a relationship, a joy, a satisfaction, a sadness, a desperation, an exhaustion. To feel close to an idea, an ideal, and to ourselves. To feel part of a country, a person and the earth. To rise out of the depths of desperation and self-made alienation, and to be close once again to you. These are what we can grasp, these are real. These are experiences. That is our prayer, Lord. To be aware, to rise up, to realize, to understand and to care.

Perhaps more than any of the others this prayer expresses one of the deepest desires of the contemporary student faced with a dismembered and broken reality in which he has to find his place, but which often seems more threatening than inviting. In a milieu that tries to refine the senses through ingenuous instruments, the student wonders if he can trust his own body and if his senses are able to bring him in contact with the reality in which he lives. But as soon as the touch of sensitivity dawns upon him a new vibration pervades him. A girl prays:

> Just to hear ... the annoying buzz of haunting alarm clocks through the thin walls of those who live nearby.
>
> Just to see ... a friend who has waited to walk with me over to class, and that look on his face when I've done it again, but I don't know what.
>
> Just to smell ... the freshness of a spring morning when the sun is warm and winter has passed: when the flowers are budding and the grass is moist.
>
> Just to feel ... the refreshment of an afternoon shower; the softness of a baby duck; the sand between my toes; the thrill of a tender kiss.
>
> Just to taste ... not only a snack or a meal, but the sweet and bitter of life; and to love with my entirety the who that they are, whether ugly or gracious or right or sad.

Students like this girl are filled with the experience of new life, new beauty and new energy. They say 'Yes' to all that is, and in their humble recognition of their own fragility they open themselves to the splendour of their beautiful God. A new ray of hope is coming through.

6. THE GIVING GOD

The antiheroic prayers showed a first hesitant appreciation of the little things. In the prayers to the compassionate God, a creative passivity became visible and the last two prayers revealed the deep desire to merge with the beautiful God and to experience a new sense of unity and belonging. We are far away from the confused state of mind, with which we started this analysis, but still not arrived at what we can call Christian hope.

The plea for sensitivity with the desire to feel deeply embedded in reality was still in many ways a plea of the lonesome, somewhat isolated man. The need to merge, to be one, to belong, often reveals a regressive impulse, which cannot tolerate the distinction between the praying man and his world, between himself and the other, between his weakness and God's strength. Often it seems as if the quest for belonging means a fear of being different and an unwillingness to claim the individuality of the self. The identity of the praying person, therefore, has not yet a clear form and a prayer for sensitivity can sound somewhat preoccupied. Its God is more a protective device than the giving other.

Obviously we only speak about differences in degree, but in the prayers to the beautiful God, God is hardly recognized as the other who is free to give or not to give. He is more an indispensable source of warmth always available to offer comfort. But once God is recognized as the other who gives in freedom, man is able to think. Sensitivity is a condition to experience God's gifts, but thanks includes also the willingness to recognize the distance between the giver and the receiver.

When man is able to thank he is able to know his limitations without feeling defensive and to be self-confident without being proud. He claims his own powers and at the same time he confesses his need for help. Thanking in a real sense avoids submissiveness as well as possessiveness. It is the act of a free man who can say: I thank you. Here I and you are two different persons with different identities who can enter in an intimate relationship without losing their own selves. An act of free thanking requires a careful balance between closeness and distance. Too much closeness can lead to a self-effacing dependency, too much distance to an overevaluation of the self with a defensive pride.

Many of the student prayers are so self-centred so full of deep personal concern, or so craving for sympathy and protection that there is not enough distance to say thanks. But there are exceptions in which a new freedom is visible and a prayer becomes a hymn of thanksgiving.

> Lord, thank You for life, love and people.

> Dear Lord, thank You for the beautiful day, for the flowers, for the birds, for my family, for my friends, for me.

> for all that has been – thanks
> for all that will be – yes!

In thanks man is open and moves outward. In confusion all the attention is drawn inward in an attempt to unravel the complexities of the internal world, hardly leaving any possibility to say thanks. In confusion man clings to himself, in thanks he stretches out his hands and points to the source of new energy, new life, new love. Thanks then can even become possible in a sad world. One student concludes a long prayer with the words:

> What can I say but thank You; in the middle of bad it has never been so good.

Here thanks can shake off the depression of the present and make hope a possibility.

THE COMING GOD

When many students were asked to read the prayers and to give their reactions to them there was an almost unanimous attraction to one prayer which we consider a prayer to the coming God. Although different students could sympathize with many strong positive or negative affects, expressed in the collection, the attitude communicated through form and content by this prayer called 'hope' was immediately recognized as the most desirable, most modern and most Christian.

I hope that I will always be for each man what he needs me to be.

I hope that each man's death will always diminish me, but that fear of my own will never diminish my joy of life.

I hope that my love for those whom I like will never lessen my love for those whom I do not.

I hope that another man's love for me never be a measure of my love for him.

I hope that every man will accept me as I am, but that I never will.

I hope that I will always ask for forgiveness from others, but will never need be asked for my own.

I hope that I will find a woman to love, but that I will never seek one.

I hope that I will always recognize my limitations, but that I will construct none.

I hope that loving will always be my goal, but that love will never be my idol.

I hope that every man will always have hope.

Here we find ourselves as far away as possible from confusion. Here we listen to a man who stands on solid ground and points into the future. He knows where he is and looks with expectation towards the things to come. The structure and thought of this prayer show a great self-confidence carefully integrated with a deep sense of humility. The prayer illustrates in a beautiful way some of the basic dynamics of the attitude of the mature Christian.

In comparison with the painful self-preoccupation, which we found in the prayer of the confused student, we see here a great sense of self-awareness, self-acceptance. There are clear, but not rigid lines which mark the personality. In this attitude of hope we see a man well defined but always available for redefinition. In comparison with the prayers to the banned God, there is no artificial rest created by a negative conversion but a free dialogue without need to defend. In hope God is no obstacle, but the way to human love. In comparison with the prayers to the big-buddy-God, there is no easy optimism nor simplistic wish-fulfilling thinking. The hope expressed is on a very personal level and never concretized in toy-like desires. Man does not ask the coming God for favours, but opens himself to a deepening of an interpersonal relationship, which depends on two persons, and can never be forced. In comparison with the antiheroic prayers to the compassionate God, there is no feeling of fatigue or reaction against an overdemanding society. In hope man does not react to a frustrating past, but reaches forward to a promising future. In comparison with the prayers to the beautiful God, the praying man here is less alienated and more self-composed. There is no desire to merge with God, but to strengthen the own identity. In hope man does not ask to vanish and lose himself in the embracing arms of a protecting God, but he experiences his being different as a creative possibility. In comparison with the prayers to the giving God, thanks is less explicitly formulated, but constantly presupposed. Real hope is impossible without the deep awareness that life is a gift and holds endless promises.

So we see in the prayer to the coming God the attitude of hope as an attitude of self-awareness and self-acceptance from which man enters in a creative dialogue with his living God, constantly leaving behind his past and stretching forward to a future which he experiences as an inexhaustible source of new life.

We tried to enter into the intimacy of the student prayerlife. We did this on invitation by studying the prayers written by the student himself and offered for evaluation. By seeing the whole collection as a move out of confusion towards mature hope we wanted to prevent ourselves from labelling the different student prayers as more or less 'good' or 'bad'. We only wanted to understand where the student could be located in his search for meaning and a God whom he can call his God. The distinctions between the different God's were perhaps too artificial, but they were intended to make it easier to recognize the intimate moves of man to come closer to himself and the God of his faith.

Pentecostalism on Campus

Since the Pentecostal movement has become a vivid reality on some university campuses, many active participants, as well as distant observers, have asked, 'Is this healthy or dangerous, something to be encouraged or something to be avoided?'

Various students who experienced the gift of tongues, who felt the Real Presence of the Holy Spirit and for whom a new world of feelings has opened itself, expressed their change: 'It is a tremendous experience. It is new, unique, full of joy and peace. I am different, that is for sure. Only one who has surrendered can really understand what I am talking about. Many problems I have long been struggling with just seemed to vanish, became like an empty shell falling off. Heavy burdens became feather-light things; hostile attitudes converted to deep sympathy. People whom I once feared are now my friends. Those whom I hated I can love, those who were masters are partners. I know with a deep certainty that God has spoken to me in a new way.'

But sometimes the same students will tell you the other side of their feelings: 'I wonder if it is all real, if it is really me. It is like another world which is not mine; one so overwhelming that it seems unreal. Once in a while, after a prayer meeting when I am by myself, I feel lonely and depressed. Will it last? Perhaps it is just for a short time and then my problems will come back. I wonder if it is really good for me.'

The same ambivalence is expressed by outsiders. They see people pray, sing, and read together; they see their happiness, joy and new convictions; but they wonder how real or healthy it is. And since this is all so close, it seems very difficult to find the distance to understand without falling into a fanatic rejection and ridicule on the one hand or an uncritical enthusiasm on the other.

This essay is an attempt to clarify certain issues and to be of some help in an honest evaluation. I will use, besides my own observations and discussions with students, the study by Kilian McDonnell, O.S.B., 'The Ecumenical Significance of the Pentecostal Movement'.[1] I will approach the subject from three perspectives.

A HISTORICAL PERSPECTIVE

Although Pentecostalism was originally found among people with a low economic status and closely related with the non-liturgical churches (such as the Assembly of God Church), since 1955 a new wave of Pentecostalism has entered the more prosperous communities, inspired many intellectuals, and established itself in such liturgical churches as the Lutheran and Episcopalian.

McDonnell, who studies the rising Pentecostalism with a group of anthropologists, is probably the most informed and knowledgeable theologian in this area. Considering it as 'the fastest growing movement within the Christian tradition'[2] he asks himself, 'How can the Pentecostals with so few means form such apostolic Christians while our liturgies rich in theological

[1] Kilian McDonnell, O.S.B. 'The Ecumenical Significance of the Pentecostal Movement' (*Worship*, December 1966).
[2] *ibid.*, p. 609.

content and tradition fail to communicate the urgency of evangelization to the faithful?' Do our liturgies develop a sense of community? Do they form a congregation which acts, prays, listens, sings and sorrows together, a true community of the redeemed? Have the Roman Catholics become comfortable with the too-oft-extolled beauties of the Roman Liturgy (sobriety, grandeur, clarity, objectivity, lapidary formulations, fixity of form, supranational appeal – the list reads as though drawn up by an enemy) and failed to notice that, in every liturgical instance and in every cultural context, sobriety and objectivity may not be virtues to emphasize, that grandeur amidst poverty may be an indictment, that supranational appeal may, in fact, be a species of Roman liturgical colonialism?

Pentecostals are in many lands the fastest-growing Christian denomination. Why? 'Undoubtedly the answer involves many factors, but this much we know. Our liturgies have failed.'[3] And McDonnell even wonders whether 'St Paul would not feel more at home in the free fervour of a Pentecostal meeting than in the organized dullness of our liturgical celebrations.'[4] There is no doubt about one thing. The rapidly growing interest in the Pentecostal prayer meeting at university-campus reveals an intensive need, a long-hidden frustration which manifests itself in the sudden breakthrough of a form of behaviour which is rather unusual in a student-community.

It is difficult to imagine how a Catholic university looked in the twenties and thirties. About the University of Notre Dame, where John F. O'Hara was the prefect of religion, Joe Hoffman writes: 'O'Hara gave Notre Dame its enormous standing within the Catholic populace of the United States as a place where the solid practice of Catholicism could be found. His goals were

[3] *ibid.*, pp. 622–623.
[4] *ibid.*, p. 615.

clear-cut and defined: Mass, Communion, frequent confession, devotion to the Blessed Sacrament and to Mary. His methods were novenas in preparation for Christmas, Easter, Mother's Day, and exams. There were processions, hours of adoration, the rosary, first Friday devotions, and all of them were popular. Freshmen arriving on campus were immediately indoctrinated into the system. By means of the Religious Bulletin, which was read as much beyond the campus as by the students, O'Hara hammered at students' foibles, suggested means for advancing in the spiritual life, gave timely notice of approaching religious events, commented on the spiritual significance of the news of the day, presented points of character development, gave short instructions on ideals, corrected student abuses, and answered difficulties. It was spiritual reading in tabloid form. O'Hara kept statistics on religious practice, published religious surveys and was keenly aware of the tempo and mentality of the student body. He was extremely successful.'[5]

Today the picture is completely different. A university is no longer a place with easygoing students who consider their four years as a relatively relaxed time with abundant opportunity for prayer, sports, social life and extracurricular activities; rather, it is a very ambitious and competitive institution. Today, students often look upon their four years as a race in which only the fittest survive. In the educational revolution of the post-Sputnik era, academic excellence became the key word.

But competition demands a price. Most students take the challenge and are able to utilize the new pressures in a useful and often creative way. But many do not, and instead they often develop an excessive amount of anxiety and tension and experience a painful loneliness which they hide beneath the surface of seemingly well-adjusted behaviour. The university

[5] Joseph Hoffman, C.S.C., unpublished article.

community now counts hundreds of very lonely men who consider their neighbours more as rivals than as friends. For many, their roommate is a stranger and their classmate a threat. 'Everyone for himself, and God for us all.' That seems most safe. Knowledge becomes a weapon by which you stay in school, avoid the Army, win a fellowship, and make a career. And the Church does not seem to help very much. Going through a time of reevaluation and extreme self-criticism, she offers more questions than answers. Instead of a safe home, she is more a source of deep discomfort for a man who looks for a solid support in a tumbling world.

In this context the Pentecostal movement very well can be understood as a revival, a rekindling of the devotional Church, or the revenge of a repressed sentiment. Everyone who enters a Pentecostal meeting is suddenly confronted with all that seems to be at odds with a 'typical' university student. In the midst of the congregation, students witness how their loneliness and insecurity have been overcome by the gift of the Holy Spirit. One who never had a friend and always felt afraid now feels free to share his deepest thoughts and desires with his fellow man. Long struggles with most embarrassing problems are wiped away by the infusion of God's Spirit. Sadness is changed to joy, restlessness to peace, despair to inner content, and separation to togetherness.

On a campus where people stay relatively distant from each other, the most intimate ideas are shared and the barriers to communication are broken. Where men hardly touch each other, they embrace and hold each other in a free physical contact. They lay lands on each other's shoulders and heads, pray aloud for each other's needs, and let themselves be led by deep spiritual impulses to which they surrender in ecstatic joy and happiness. The new feelings are so great and overpowering that they cannot be caught in human concepts or words, but break through in ecstatic sounds varying in tone and intensity and expressing a prayer of total surrender and praise, saying with Jeremiah, 'Ah, Lord, I don't know how to speak'. Hands, eyes and mouth express unknown happiness, openness and joy. Young men move up and down in the pleasant rhythm of biblical songs, or are quiet in a long and contemplative silence. So intense is the exchange that many feel a new, warm intensity pervading their whole persons. Their hands radiate new power and a soft and tender breeze touches their skins. Joy and happiness may break through in tears and sweat and the intensity of the prayer may lead to a happy and satisfying experience of physical exhaustion caused by total surrender.

The Spirit has come. He who asks will receive and feel that God is not a strange God. He will taste again His sweetness, hear His internal call, and be able to love Him with his whole person, body and soul, without any reservation.

A PSYCHOLOGICAL PERSPECTIVE

How can we evaluate this new movement? We can understand it as a revival of the devotional Church and as a reaction of a repressed religious sentiment in a cool and competitive world. But is it healthy or sick? Does it cure or make wounds? It is very difficult to give an outright answer, but perhaps some considerations may be of help.

Does it heal or hurt? There is no doubt that many people who surrendered to this experience get a tremendous and often very sudden relief from their mental and spiritual pains. Problems they have been struggling with for years are wiped away in a moment and lose their unbearable weight. The questions are: Are they cured or covered? Is the real human conflict resolved or 'snowed under' by the overwhelming power of a new experience?

109

We know that electroshock, an artificially induced emotional experience, can cover a depression for many years but does not cure it. It may make us forget our problems for some years, but, in fact, it delays the process of cure by not using the human qualities to heal. One might wonder if the miraculous effect of the Pentecostal experience is not in a certain way like a shock treatment. If a young man or woman suddenly feels redeemed from deep mental suffering, they might, in fact, paralyze their internal human ability to overcome their problem, and when the pains recur later on they might be more discouraged than before.

If we use sleeping pills, we certainly will fall asleep but, at the same time, we can kill our own capacities to find physical rest and become quite dependent on these external forces. And, if the Pentecostal experience in many cases gives this sudden freedom, sudden friendship, sudden happiness and joy, we might prevent the gradual development of our internal capacities to develop meaningful, lasting friendships, to enjoy happiness, and to tolerate frustrations. Many people who have had deep, internal religious experiences (during retreats, cursillos, novitiates, etc.) all can witness to the fact that they relieved many pains for a while, but that the real test came later when there were no feelings to depend on, no experiences to count on. The task lies in the desert where God is not feelable and naked faith is all we have.

The Pentecostal experience might take away (even permanently) certain real problems, but it is very doubtful that it will cure deep mental suffering. It might only cover it up and delay the attempt for a real cure.

Can it be dangerous? For many people, perhaps even for most, it hardly seems to be dangerous. It might be even beneficial to a certain extent, especially for those who through retreats, cursillos and other religious practices have become exposed to the inner feelings that are in line with the Pentecostal experience. But for some it is dangerous – very dangerous.

First of all, for those who are not prepared, every inducement of a strong emotion can break and do serious harm. The Christian tradition has been deeply convinced of the importance of preparation. Christ did not come to this world before a long preparation of His people. We do not celebrate Christmas without Advent, nor Easter without Lent. And St Paul distinguishes between Christians who still need spiritual milk and those who are ready for solid food. The whole mystical tradition stresses the need for purification in order to enter into intimacy with God and the danger of unprepared exposure to divine powers.

Several students showed remarkable signs of anxiety and confusion. They were so overwhelmed by these new feelings that they lost their hold on reality. They found they could no longer study nor concentrate on their daily work; they felt a pushing urge to share with others. In some cases, physical and mental exhaustion were visible, and people felt on the edge of a physical or mental breakdown. This is dangerous and may lead to psychotic reaction, which needs hospitalization and special psychiatric help in order to be cured. These are exceptional cases, but still no less a source of concern.

Secondly, there are those who strongly desire to have the gifts of the Spirit but do not feel able to come to the real experience. They wonder why others are so happy, and they are not; why others can speak in tongues and they cannot; why others feel free to embrace each other, and they do not. More than ever before, they feel like outsiders or even outcasts. And they wonder, 'What is wrong with me that I do not receive the gifts?' Feelings of guilt and depression can result from this, and many may feel more lonely than before. For those who ask but do not receive, the Pentecostal movement can create real dangers.

There is a heavy responsibility on the leaders of the movement. Emotion, and certainly religious emotions, need careful direction, careful guidance, and careful care.

Does it create community? Who could deny this? The free and easy way in which the participants relate to each other, talk, sing and pray together should convince everybody that here a real, new community is formed. Still there are some questions here. By suddenly breaking through the barriers of shyness and distance, many have given away their privacy. Many have shown their deepest self to their fellow man and laid themselves open for the other. They have stripped themselves of their reservations and inhibitions and have shared their most intimate feelings, ideas and thoughts with others. In a way they have merged their personality with their friends and given up their otherness.

But, is this real community? One who has given away so much of himself creates an unquenchable need to be constantly together with the other to whom he has given himself, in order to feel a whole person. Many students who actively participated in the prayer meetings felt terribly lonely during the vacation and felt a deep urge and desire to be with their friends again. Instead of creating the freedom to leave the group and to go out and work, many want to remain in the safe protection of the togetherness where they can really feel at home.

The lack of distance and the stress on intimacy make the creative community hardly possible. A good liturgy should always be characterized by a subtle balance between closeness and distance. It should offer different modes and levels of participation and many ways of religious experience. Perhaps it seldom did before and is only thought of as a distant, cool reality. But in the Pentecostal movement on campus, closeness has become so central that there is little room left for those who want to retain some distance and keep an intimacy for themselves.

In this context the danger is real that the Pentecostal movement creates a situation in which there is a growing desire to reinforce the feelings of oneness and togetherness, which makes the community highly self-centred and hinders the development of the autonomous Christian who does not depend on the other to feel his own commitments. A real community is for stretching out. The Pentecostal community tends to be bent over inwards, and, without so wanting or aspiring, to become an in-group, developing the idea of a spiritual elite (as the cursillo did) with a subtle handling of the terms 'we' and 'they'.

Are the prayer meetings all spontaneous? The informal, somewhat casual character of the Pentecostal meetings suggests that the real leadership is given to the Holy Spirit. But on closer observation, the meetings are found to be much more organized. There is a certain programme that reappears in most Pentecostal meetings: First, witnesses, songs, readings, which prepare for the baptism of the Spirit. Then there is some time allotted for free conversation in which people share their experiences. Finally, after offering more prayers, songs and readings, the laying on of the hands takes place, leading to a climax in the speaking in tongues and the praising of the Lord in ecstatic forms of happiness and joy. This all could not take place without strong and very influential leaders.

But here a new question arises. Who accepts responsibility or authority? The 'leaders' refer immediately to the Spirit as the great leader. To the question 'Can't the experience be very dangerous for some people?' they would reply, 'The Holy Spirit cannot do dangerous things. He is a healing force.' In this way the 'leaders' refuse explicit leadership, responsibility and authority, confiding in the immediate intervention of God. But in so doing they tend to neglect a definite responsibility, not only in terms of preparation and the actual event but also in terms of the long-range consequences that these experiences will have on the

113

ongoing development of the spiritual life of the people involved.

A THEOLOGICAL PERSPECTIVE

An active participant of the Pentecostal movement will probably pay very little attention to a psychological approach to his experience. He might even feel psychology to be a hindrance to the free movements of the Spirit.

But this immediately raises the question of the theological significance of the Pentecostal movement. Most remarkable is the conviction of the immediate intervention of the Holy Spirit in human life. During the meetings the 'leaders' often explain how he who is willing to surrender and ask for God's coming will experience the eruption of the Spirit in this human world and allow Him to take over the initiative. 'Pentecostalism was, and to a degree remains, more a movement than a church,' McDonnell has said.[6] We cannot speak about a Pentecostal doctrine, and perhaps it is for this reason that Pentecostalism so easily becomes a part of different religious institutions to which it adapts itself quite easily. For entering the Catholic Church, Pentecostalism could establish contact at the sacramental level by showing 'the relation of the sacramental life to personal holiness and practical piety'.[7]

It is, therefore, understandable that Pentecostalism brings people back to their religious practices. Often students who did not 'practise their religion' return to confession, Communion, and their lost devotion to Our Lady and the rosary. In no way does Pentecostalism seem to threaten the Catholic orthodoxy.

[6] Kilian McDonnell, O.S.B., *op. cit.*, p. 623.
[7] *ibid.*, p. 621.

The opposite seems true. In the eyes of many, it seems to point to a reinforcing of the basic Roman Catholic doctrines and beliefs.

But it is exactly here where many theologians raise questions. For, while not denying any Catholic doctrine or practice, the Pentecostals within the Catholic Church act in a way which does not take into account the major development of the recent renewal in Catholic theology. A deeper understanding of the incarnation leads to a rethinking of the humanity of God. More and more it has become clear that God reveals Himself to man through man and his world and that a deeper understanding of human behaviour leads us to a deeper understanding of God. The new insights of psychology, sociology, anthropology and so forth are no longer feared as possible threats to the supernatural God, but more as an invitation to theological reflection on the new insights and understandings. Vatican II strongly supported this humanization of the Church, and the new theology was a great encouragement to mobilize all the human potentialities in the different levels of human life as being the most authentic way to understand the voice of God to His people. The new theology was 'discovered' by a deeper understanding of the createdness of the world, by discerning that there is a task of Christian secularization. It was exactly this that the first Christians did: demythologize Caesar and the State. The more we make the world what it ought to be, a created reality with tremendous potentialities for growth, the more this world calls for Him, who is Uncreated. And in this sense secularization is possible only by faith.

In the perspective of this trend in theology, which also encourages more social action and 'worldly' involvement, the Pentecostal trend seems a step back. It calls for God's immediate intercession outside the human potentials. In a way it seems that God does not use man, unless as a passive instrument which is the victim of the struggle between demonic and divine forces. The devil is an alien power invading man, and so is the Spirit. The question then becomes, 'Who is possessing me?' But possession, good or evil, remains a passive state; it does not give full credit to the basic Christian idea that we are created to create, and to realize our deepest human potentialities in the service of our fellow men, in the love of whom we discover the Spirit of God.

Having discussed the Pentecostal movement as a revival of the devotional Church, as a religious reaction to a world with a heavy stress on achievement, and as raising many psychological and theological questions, the critical tone might have over-shadowed a deeper concern about a valid religious experience. We might have overlooked that in one way the Pentecostal movement is an invitation to a deeper search. It made God a living God, a real experience, an actual event. Whereas the whole field of theological education is desperately looking for ways to bring theology from 'brain level to guts level', the Pentecostals certainly do it. And it is no surprise that many envy those who experience the presence of God as an undeniable reality. Is it not just this that all the forms of renewal (liturgical, social, clerical, etc.) are trying to do – make religious life some-thing vibrant, a living source of constant inspiration?

The new wave of Pentecostalism on campus obviously answers a burning need in many students. It worries many who are concerned about the effects on the mental health of some of the participants, it places a heavy responsibility on the leaders of the movement, and it disturbs many theologians; but it also offers a chance to come to a new realization of the crucial importance of valid religious experience as an authentic part of the Christian life. It would be a pity if we missed this chance by a hasty judgment and an intolerant condemnation.

Intimacy and Community

Depression in the Seminary

It is not too long ago that the stereotype of the seminarian offered the picture of a very nice, sweet boy, somewhat talkative, easily excited about such innocent things as a recent article, naive, inexperienced especially in matters of sex, but always good-natured, friendly, smiling, and ready to help even when not asked.

That stereotype is changing rapidly. What we see today is far from an easy-going, optimistic young man. We are struck by quite different characteristics. We are more likely to find a problem-ridden, struggling student who takes himself, his world and his future very seriously, who wants to debate and discuss many issues, who is seldom relaxed, but inclined to experience his youth as a long and dark tunnel the end of which he does not see.

And whereas we tended to think of the seminary as a place with joyful, self-confident people, now a visitor might find it to be a place with troubled, doubting people, pervaded with a general atmosphere of depression. Although we are stereotyping and therefore simplifying, we cannot avoid the growing conviction that depression is one of the most surprising symptoms in our seminary communities. If it is true that depression is considered as one of the main problems of the college student, this is even more the case if we consider the seminarian of today. For not only a distant look but even many intensive discussions with seminarians leave one with the feeling that a heavy cloud, undefined and mysterious, is darkening the life of the seminary.

And many staff members find themselves amazed and deeply disappointed when they discover that after years of conscious modernization and liberalization, after many efforts to open a closed system, to free an unfree institution, they find their students sad instead of happy, unfriendly and moody instead of good-natured, closed and suspicious instead of open and communicative. This seemingly strange phenomenon demands our special attention today. Our main question is: What is the relationship between formation and depression? And, as no clinician will ever advise any therapeutic measure without a careful and specific diagnosis, we will first try to understand the nature of the depression and its correlation with different new techniques in formation. Then we will try to make some suggestions which might help us in our task to overcome this painful and often destructive symptom.

I. DIAGNOSTIC CONSIDERATIONS

There is no doubt that we who are seminary staff members find ourselves in a very complex situation, actually in the middle of a paradox. We are giving to people who come to us for information the freedom to educate themselves. We are taking away structures from people who want to be formed through channelling their unstructured drives. We have become deeply convinced that the highly regimented seminary life belongs definitely to the past, but also we have discovered that many new freedoms do not always give the desired satisfaction. In this context we have to face the problem of seminary depression.

Intimacy

I propose to discuss this problem in two ways: as a problem of identity for the students and staff, and as a problem of new educational methods.

[a] Depression as an identity problem
1. A problem of student identity

Staff-members are dealing with students who realize that they have not yet fully developed their potential, who experience a tremendous amount of energy, and who have only a vague idea in which direction they want to go. The students all hope to find three things:

[a] Competence, which enables them to cope with the demands of society.
[b] Control, which provides them with channels for their unruly impulses.
[c] Vocation, which gives them the conviction that they are called to do what they felt vaguely attracted to.

Some will discover that they are not intelligent enough to become competent, some will find that their deepest desires point in a direction other than celibate community life, and many will recognize that they are not called for the work they felt inclined to in the beginning. But it is certain that all are looking for a structure, clear, explicit and articulated, in which they can test themselves and be tested by others in order to allow the necessary decisions for their future life. If this is true we immediately become aware of a severe identity crisis in terms of competence, impulse control and vocation.

[a] If a seminarian wants competence he finds himself involved in one of the most difficult fields to feel competent in –

theology. The questions of theology vary from questions regarding specific issues all the way to the question of whether theology is a field for study at all. Very few students feel proud of theology as their discipline in the way a lawyer, doctor, sociologist, or psychologist is proud of his field, and most often they hope to become competent in other areas of study besides theology in order to feel like valuable members of society.

[b] If a seminarian wants to find control for his strong drives and impulses, he finds himself in a situation where many taboos are questioned and in which he finds many ambiguous signals regarding the expression of his erotic desires. What has vanished is clarity. A student who pronounced temporary vows and dates a girl on the side is not expelled from the seminary, but rather it is suggested to him in many ways that it might be good to have some dating experience before he makes up his mind. Not too long ago the so-called 'particular friendships' were a subject of concern to many faculty members, and of ridicule to the students who did not really know what their superiors were so concerned about. But today the staff has become afraid to even warn against particular friendships whereas many students find themselves in energy-devouring personal relationships with roommates or friends and are sometimes made very anxious due to the obvious sexual feelings which have come to their awareness. Overt homosexual relations which ten years ago were mostly a part of the fantasy of the staff now at times have become a part of the student's problems.

[c] If a student comes to deepen his vocation, he finds that hardly anybody can tell him what it means to be a priest. We might even say that the closer he comes to ordination the

121

vaguer his ideas about the priesthood become. When he entered the seminary, he perhaps wanted to be a man like his uncle-priest, his teacher-priest, or like one of the priests he admired, but while going through the years of formation he is exposed to so much questioning, doubting and personal failures that he starts wondering more and more if he should give the most explicit unchangeable commitment to the most undefined and unclear profession. At the same time he wonders who is calling whom. Ten years ago it was clear that the church called and that it was an honour, privilege and election to be ordained to the priesthood. The representatives of the church made it clear: 'If you don't live up to the expectations, we ask you to leave.' But now the student seems to say to the church: 'If you don't live up to my expectations I am leaving.' And in many subtle ways it is communicated to the student that nobody wants to lose him and that he can make more demands on the church than the church on him. And although it might seem that this form of student power is attractive to the seminarian, the fact of the matter is that nobody wants to enter a profession which does not contain a demanding call.

So we see that precisely in the three main areas of seminary formation, Competence, Control and Vocation, the student feels frustrated. He feels like a man without a respected discipline, surrounded by ambiguous signals concerning his impulse control and preparing himself for a vocation which has become subject to endless questioning. Slowly the idea crawls up to him that the most unpopular thing to do these days is to become a priest. For a young man, full of energy, ambition and generosity, commitment to an unappreciated, nonchallenging and unclear life seems no commitment at all. And it is not difficult to see that this identity crisis can become the source of a painful depression.

2. A problem of staff identity

The problem, however, is not just a student problem. The new attitudes of the faculty also explain part of this strange feeling of a collective depression. In a somewhat complicated and seldom recognized way, the democratization of student-faculty relations cause unexpected conflicts. Not too long ago seminaries were places with many rules, usually strict observance and a clear-cut division of authority. There was a lot of rebellion and anger caused by this structure, but students knew to whom to show their anger and against whom to rebel. There was usually a clear system of reward and punishment and students knew what to expect when they took a risk and were caught in the act – frequently a very innocent act of trespassing some quite irrelevant rule. But then someone came to them and said: 'It is up to you, if you want to go to Mass or not, if you want to stay in bed or not, go to parties or not, date girls or not, stay up all night or not, come to the recreation or not. You know what you are supposed to do. It is up to your own conscience to do it.' Most good, willing and idealistic staff members don't always see what this means. Many times it simply means, 'We expect you to do all these things and follow all these rules, but we will not enforce them. We trust you and your own judgment. We hope you won't disappoint us.'

The result of this new attitude is the situation of sin without the possibility of doing penance. Seminarians now act in many ways which they know that their superiors don't like, but nobody says anything, nobody objects, reprimands or punishes. They only look disappointed, personally offended, and are saying with their eyes: 'I thought I could trust you, but now you do this to me.' If a man has nobody to punish him when he feels he deserves it, he starts punishing himself. It is this inward-turned hostility which causes the depression which has become such a pervasive mood in many seminarians. And many staff members

are surprised and even bitterly disappointed that all their generous gifts of freedom to the students are not accepted with a joyful thanks, but result in an often loaded and chokingly unfree
student-staff relationship. We should take a closer look at this
phenomenon. Two aspects seem important: a) The personalized
punishment, and b) The verbal and non-verbal communication
of doubts.

[a] The personalized punishment

The staff very often is disappointed that the students don't live
up to the expectations. Students prove less generous than the
faculty hoped. They take advantage of their new freedom, do
not express thanks for it, but only ask for more. Superiors and
other faculty members very often feel personally hurt, and
although their hands are itching to slap the student in the face,
they feel too liberal to do so, and have to resort to a very subtle
and often harmful form of punishment, such as: speaking about
lack of trust, sudden inappropriate anger about very small
things, looking sombre and heavy, and communicating on a
very personal level that they are offended and that the students
make their life miserable. And just as no child can adequately
react to his mother who instead of punishing the child for
breaking a glass, says, 'Don't you love mama more than to do
this to me?', so a student does not know how to handle this
highly personalized form of punishment. He can only feel guilty
and unable to do anything about it. And that is what creates this
tense and choking feeling which takes the humour out of relationships and makes everyone hypersensitive to each other.

[b] Communication of doubts

The second aspect of the student-staff relationship which can
lead to depression is the way in which the staff communicates
its own problems. Many faculty members are questioning the

same basic values the student are questioning. They realize that the student problems are not just problems related to their own individual growing pains, but to the growing pains of the whole church. And many seminary teachers are doubting if it is good to encourage a young, intelligent man to become a priest in a community full of confusion and worries. They are asking themselves: 'Am I really making a man happy by encouraging him to persevere in the seminary? Can I really give a meaningful answer to his question of what it means to be a priest in a modern world? Does it really make sense to advise him to commit himself for life to a status in which sexual intimacy cannot be striven for? Can I take the responsibility, even when it is a partial responsibility, for anybody's choice of a profession which is in the middle of drastic change?'

These doubts and this anguish do not remain unnoticed by students. In many verbal and nonverbal ways these existential questions enter into the student-faculty relationship. Identification is still the main process by which a man finds his vocation in life. Strong convincing personalities, who give an attractive visibility to their way of life, are the most powerful influences on a young man's life choice. Who wants to become a doctor when his teachers don't believe that they can cure, who wants to be coached by a coach who does not believe that he can win a game, who wants to become a teacher when his professor is only bitter about his students? And who wants to become a priest if he lives with priests who question the foundations of their commitment: the nature of the priesthood, the church, the incarnation and the concept of God. And although these questions are not always personal questions, they are so much a part of the general atmosphere of religious life today that only a stubborn isolationist can completely stay away from them.

Therefore we might wonder if many faculty members who encourage their students to discuss their problems in an open exchange of ideas and adopt the role of understanding listeners themselves, do not in fact, although not intentionally, pass on their burden. And students might experience this as if they are told: 'You might like to have a try at the problems which we did not find an answer for ourselves.' It might even be possible that many forms of liberalization in today's seminary formation are felt by the students to be testimony of the incapacity to offer meaningful structures on the side of the staff. Many seminarians, who have participated in year-long discussions on about every possible basic subject are showing signs of fatigue, disappointment, confusion and even hostility. Some even feel cheated, as if they had wasted their time groping with questions which don't lead anywhere and are doomed to create frustration.

And so we find not only depression related to the identity crisis of the students but also related to the identity crisis of the staff. It is exactly the mutual reinforcement of many doubts, uncertainties and worries which makes it so difficult to lift the hovering cloud above the seminary. If we now will try to analyze some of the new trends in seminary formation we have to try to understand the temptation of creating a vicious circle of depression which is very difficult to break.

[b] Depression and the new educational methods

Having discussed the seminary depression as a problem of identity of students as well as staff members, we now should have a closer look at some new educational techniques to explore their possible relationships with this phenomenon. We will limit our discussion to two new approaches in seminary education which have become very popular in practically all modern seminaries in the United States as well as in Europe: I will call them dialogue and small-group living. And although you might experience it as a rather painful process, I propose to analyze these new methods in some detail to show some of the most over-looked complications of these methods. It might be important to say at this point that I do not try in any way to question or minimize the value of these methods. I only hope to point out the many hidden traps of which we have to be aware in order to avoid them.

1. Dialogue and depression

The word dialogue is used here in a very general way. It is meant to embrace many forms of behaviour described in terms such as: encounter, open discussion, talking things through, being open to each other, and it indicates a high level of verbal communication. In this analysis we want to focus on the verbal aspects of the dialogue.

The growing emphasis on the value of verbal communication of students with each other and their faculty is based on two usually unarticulated presuppositions which are usually taken for granted. They are, first, that free and open sharing of ideas and feelings brings people closer together, and, secondly, that a high degree of verbal interchange facilitates existential decisions by clarifying the issues involved.

Our first question therefore is: Does verbal communication bring people closer together? Although words are meant to communicate, they very often are used as a curtain to prevent communication. You probably remember that one of the best ways to succeed in an oral exam is to keep talking to prevent the professor from asking more questions, or to keep him talking, allowing him to suggest the answer before you have to confess your ignorance. In many discussions words are used to fill a fearful silence, to prevent the real questions from being asked or the painful issues from being touched. Many parliamentary discussions are aimed more at delaying the problem than at coping with it. Hours of talk in the United Nations, which to an

Intimacy

outsider seem trivial and artificial, fulfill the highly useful function of preventing a dangerous encounter. Although this seems obvious on a large scale we seldom are aware of these same dynamics if we encourage our students to discuss their problems. But let us not forget that students who are constantly subject to grading and evaluation are in many ways afraid of each other and usually hyper-self-conscious. They are often so caught up in questioning their own adequacy that they are hardly open to allowing anybody to enter into the sensitive area of their personality, where they experience doubts and confusions. When you observe a discussion of students carefully, you will often find yourselves in the midst of many verbal harnesses, which are often more restraining the more words are used. If you don't believe it, just see what happens when someone is interrupted. The only one who usually brings the subject back to the moment of interruption is the speaker himself. Very seldom someone else says: 'Sorry, you were talking about your trip through the mountains when John came in. How did things go on?' If the storyteller himself does not pick up the subject again, the conversation shifts to other subjects without pain.

What do people do when others are speaking? Well, very often they are busy preparing their own story, or deciding upon their own position. If someone remarks: 'The assassination of Senator Kennedy was the result of a communist conspiracy', the usual reaction to that statement is the internal question: 'Do I agree or not?' Instead of trying to better understand the speaker's position, the listener is thrown back on himself, and is busy figuring out his own position. And as soon as this position is verbally expressed, the rest of the dialogue is often a constant attempt to defend it, and to avoid defeat. Very often you will see people convincing themselves and their peers of an idea which they only hesitantly formulated in the beginning. The sadness of this story is that people often enter the discussion freely and relatively open-minded, and leave it very opinionated, with the meagre satisfaction that they could not be convinced of the opposite and that they won a battle even when there was basically nothing to win.

All I am trying to say is that verbal interchange between students does not always bring them closer together. It might just as well separate them. Seminarians who have been encouraged to dialogue with the suggestion that this will create a better community can become very disappointed and even hostile when they find that a year of discussion did not take away their feelings of loneliness and alienation. Often enough they find an unexpected contrast between the result of many discussions and the main reason why they engaged themselves in the first place. And sometimes they feel more like strangers after than before the dialogue started. It is not difficult to see how a feeling of failure and depression can come forth from this experience.

Our second question is: How far does the clarification of pertinent issues help to solve existential problems? Here we touch a very painful source of frustration. For insight into a problem and the ability to cope with it are two different things. If seminarians discuss the meaning of the priesthood, celibacy, the institutional church, the death of God, etc., this might help them to think more clearly about these issues and to see the different ramifications of the problems, but if they expect to solve their very personal questions: Should I become a priest, live a celibate life, remain within the institutional church, and believe in a living God? then long discussions can become an excruciating experience. I have followed a year-long discussion by seminarians who hoped to make a decision on celibacy before the approaching date of the ordination. It was sad to see how these students became more and more entangled in a complex net of arguments, ideas and concepts and found themselves lost in a labyrinth of theological turnpikes, highways and sideroads, with a growing anger that they never came to that mysterious centre where the answer was supposed to lie waiting for them.

What is really happening here? What would you think about a boy and a girl spending an hour a day to find convincing arguments that they love each other? You know these discussions are the best argument that they should not marry each other, if they don't want to enter into a rigid, stiff relationship, with a total lack of spontaneity.

Discussion requires a certain distance from the subject which allows you to see the many aspects of the issues, and gives you the opportunity to be analytical about it. But analysis means a temporary delay of participation. And only on the level of participation, existential decisions are made. Nobody becomes a priest because of three or four convincing arguments. Nobody commits himself to the celibate life because of Rahner, Schillebeeckx or Sydney Callahan. Theology, psychology and sociology don't offer solutions for existential crises, and everyone who suggests this enhances frustration, especially in the case of young men who have not yet fully experienced the limitation of the ratio.

There is a tragic and humorous note to the fact that, whereas in many seminaries there is a growing adoration for explicit intellectual awareness and an increasing emphasis on 'knowing what you do,' the nonreligious youth is burning incense, practising meditation, and eating seed, to reach a higher degree of participation with the basic sources of life. Meanwhile our liturgies have become more talkative and verbose, and incense and other stimuli, auditory and visual, are scorned as being a part of an old magic.

But what we see is that the seminarians feel caught in the ropes of their dialogues and, seeing no end in terms of decision-making, they become disappointed, moody and depressed.

2. Small group living and depression

Besides a growing emphasis on dialogue and discussion we find in many formation programmes a shift from large, sometimes anonymous, groups of students living together in one building, to the more intimate, small groups, which often are called teams.

The team approach is an obvious reaction to a very impersonal kind of living in which the students went through many years of formation without ever being able to establish meaningful relationships with their fellow students or faculty. By dividing the large group into small teams, the possibility of real fraternities is created and a new form of community living envisioned. But here also, just as in the case of dialogue and discussion, things don't always work out in the expected direction. Let us try to understand some of the difficulties involved with the team approach.

[a] The first problem is the simple fact that seminarians cannot avoid each other any longer. In a large group, where small, informal subgroups usually develop, there exists the possibility of staying away from irritating people, of keeping distant from others who seem to operate on a different wavelength, and of moving more or less freely in and out. In a team you are very close to a few fellows, and many of your activities are under the critical eyes of your team members, even when you don't feel attracted to them. If you do not show up at a team meeting, this not only will be noticed, but also criticized as a sign of lack of interest or commitment to the group. If you do not speak in a gathering people wonder why you are so silent. Whatever you do or don't do can become highly charged by very personal connotations. It is obvious therefore that team living is much more demanding than living in a large group, and asks for a much greater maturity.

[b] The second problem is related to the confusion about the meaning of a team. The word team is usually used to indicate the cooperation of a small group of people who by coordination of their different skills are better able to fulfil a certain task. The common task is what determines the nature of the team. If the team does not function well, this will be reflected in the quality of the work.

In a formation setting, however, the team often is not task-oriented. The team wants to create the best possible living conditions for its members. It is more like a family unit to which you return after a busy day of work. And here the problems start, because the team in this setting easily becomes self-oriented instead of task-oriented, and the problems of the team are not any longer related to questions raised by the nature of the work to be done but to questions raised by the nature of the interpersonal relationships. And in this case many team meetings tend to degenerate into amateur group therapy, in which members try to explore their feelings towards each other, and encourage each other to put on the table many things which much better could remain in the drawer. Team meetings in this case can become highly charged, and instead of moving away from individual concerns to a common concern, they can become self-centred to the point of narcissism.

We have to realize that the students involved are already very self-conscious, considering their age, their academic life and their ambivalent feelings towards their future profession. And although it might be very important that individual anxiety and confusion be expressed at certain times, the main purpose of the whole formation is to encourage students to grow away from this self-interest and to become free and open, to be really interested in the life and concerns of their fellowmen.

It is true that a culture which does not allow regression at times can ruin people. Without sleep man cannot live, but the real things usually don't happen during sleep. Crying, talking about yourself, and defenceless expression of feelings of love and hate are very important for the mental health of man, but they all are temporary regressions which can only be meaningful in terms of an ensuing progression. In formation regression should be allowed and even encouraged at times, but never considered as an ideal to strive for. The ideal remains not to be concerned with yourself, not to cry, not to express all your emotions, but to forget your own problems, and to do the work which calls for your attention and interest. Therefore, I feel that a team in which regressive forms of behaviour are encouraged is vitiating its own purpose.

[c] This brings us to the final problem with the team, which is related to intimacy. Loneliness is often experienced on a very deep and painful level by adolescents and young adults. The tendency exists to look for a solution to this problem by establishing very demanding and often exhausting friendships. These friendships can be clinging and immature and based on primitive needs. One of the tasks of formation is to stimulate the student not to let himself be guided by these impulsive needs, but to come to a mature self-awareness and self-confidence, in which friendship can develop as a giving and forgiving relationship and in which feelings of loneliness can be understood and accepted in a mature way.

Therefore it is very important to prevent the team from becoming a clique which is allowed to act on primitive needs and desires. This is difficult because the stresses on many students are so intense that they often have inexhaustible needs for intimacy, and clinging friendships. But this is often encouraging the unrealistic fantasy that the true, real, faithful friend is somewhere waiting, able to take away all the feelings of frustration. A man who lives in the seminary or enters the priesthood with

133

this fantasy is doomed to be a very unhappy man. And if the team becomes a way to satisfy this unrealistic desire for intimacy, much harm can be done.

So we can see that team living is a very special and delicate enterprise which demands the special attention of those who are responsible for formation. The main danger is that a task-oriented team degenerates into a self-oriented clique in which sticky relationships drain the psychic energy of the students and allow regressive behaviour. In this situation students easily become peevish, very demanding and irritable. They tend to ask for more attention than anybody can give and for more sympathy than anybody can show. They speak more about love than is healthy, enjoy in a very subtle way their own loneliness, and show basically all the symptoms of a spoiled child. And the most common universal and contagious symptom of this regressive behaviour is depression, the feeling of not being understood, loved or liked, and the desire to be pitied by those for whom they feel a strange mixture of hostility and love. And so small-group living can easily, in complete contrast with its intention, degenerate into a very depressing way of living. Most remarkable is that the feelings involved are often so vague and all-pervasive that the seminarians themselves and even the staff have great difficulty in identifying the source of the problem.

Appendix: The problem of fatigue

Before finishing this diagnostic section, I would like to consider one of the most visible symptoms related to the problem of dialogue and small-group living. A remarkable number of seminarians complain about an inappropriate degree of fatigue. Although they can sleep as long as they want, they look very tired. Their eyelids feel heavy and they experience their bodies as something they carry around. The philosopher might say:

'They have their bodies more than they are their bodies.' When they wake up in the morning they don't feel relaxed, but are very much aware of themselves lying on the bed as a heavy load. Even dressing becomes like a job that asks for concentration and special energy. This so-called neurotic fatigue is the result of a way of living which is characterized by hyperawareness, by which man does not rely any longer on his automatic processes, but wants to know what he does from moment to moment. Just as a man who wants to be aware of his breathing is in danger, and one who wants to control his heartbeat cannot live, a seminarian who speaks all the time about friendship, love and community might miss the opportunity to experience any of these realities. This lack of participating life is usually related to an often unconscious anxiety. Somehow man in that state of fatigue has temporarily lost his basic confidence that life is good and worth living and acts as if he has to be constantly awake, always prepared for unexpected traps and dangers.

This form of fatigue can be harmful because it easily brings the students into a vicious circle which he can hardly break. His depression makes him tired, and his fatigue makes him depressed, and so on. I do not want to suggest that all or most seminarians show this symptom, but some of them do, and recognizing its nature might prevent us from saying: 'Come on, take a good rest and don't study for a day,' because instead of helping him, that sort of advice might make it worse.

This finishes our diagnostic section, in which we discussed the problem of depression as a problem of identity of students and staff and as a problem related to the new educational methods, dialogue and small-group living. As an often visible symptom of depression, we focused on the neurotic fatigue. All this leaves us with many questions. The temptation now is to say: 'Perhaps we should go back to the good old days, with the early hours, long meditation, the rites of discipline and the whole clearcut system of reward and punishment.' Before we make that mistake we should raise the question of therapy.

2. THERAPEUTIC CONSIDERATION

After our rather long diagnosis we might wonder if the new trends in seminary education are really as promising as we hoped them to be. If openness to many basic questions, the new democratic forms of government, the emphasis on dialogue and small-group living result in a funereal atmosphere or a collection of intelligent grumpies, we could become somewhat suspicious about being modern.

But this is a temptation, the famous temptation, of using the weak spots in renewal as an argument for conservatism. If anything is clear it is that the seminary life as we knew it ten years ago is gone, never to return. And what is even more clear is that it took courage, imagination, and a great sensitivity to our changing world to start new ways in the preparation for the priesthood and the religious life. And it would be easy, cheap and dishonest to point to the mistakes of those who took the risks of new experiments. Every form of experimentation is bound to yield some unexpected problems. If they were expected, it probably was not a real experiment to begin with.

But we also have to try to account for the problems. And when we explained how new student-staff relationships and new educational approaches have their painful drawbacks, we did not want to suggest that the new ways are the wrong ways, but that they can perhaps be smoothed a little bit by a better understanding of the dynamics involved.

Therefore, our task now is to formulate an 'antidepressive regime', that is, guidelines which might help to alleviate the depressive reactions to many creative initiatives. Before mentioning, however, any specific guidelines we should formulate the principle on which all guidelines rest. That principle is that all formation has as its primary task to offer a meaningful structure which allows for a creative use of the student's energies. Structure is the key word of formation and the criterion of any educational guideline. Structure allowing one to judge which feelings to trust and which feelings to distrust, which ideas to follow and which to reject. Structure providing unity to the many seemingly disconnected emotions and ideas of the student. Structure which helps to decide which plan is just a fancy and which contains the seed for a workable project. Structure, which offers the possibility to organize the day, plan the year, and steer the course of life.

Our problems today are not related to the fact that we are too modern, too liberal or too progressive, but that we do not have as yet the meaningful structures through which we can help the student give form to his many as yet undirected and unfocused potentialities.

In the context of this principle we now will try to formulate some guidelines. We will do this in terms of student-faculty identity and in terms of the new educational methods.

[a] Structure and the identity problem

A student who is struggling with his identity in terms of competence, control and vocation will never find this if the staff to whom he daily relates does not claim in a clear and defined way its own role. This role is a role of authority. If a staff member has no authority at all a student cannot relate to him as a student. The main guideline here is that the staff has to be authoritative without becoming authoritarian. Authoritative simply means that the source of the staff member's authority lies in his

137

competence, maturity and faith. He knows his field, is able to cope with the tensions of life and believes that he is called to do a meaningful work. This is the kind of authority that is inner-directed and does not need to rely on quotes from popes, bishops or superiors in order to give a sense to desires. An authoritarian man needs the rules to live, an authoritative man lives in such a way that the rules become obvious. Students want to be criticized, reprimanded and even punished. They ask for it if you can hear their language. But the authority by which this happens should be based not on subjective feelings and ideas, not on abstract rules and regulations, but on a critical, competent and objective understanding of the students' behaviour.

Conflicts, frictions and differences of opinion don't have to be avoided. They are a part of formation. But only when the faculty claims its own authority and insists on it, will the student be able to identify himself, evaluate his own experiments in life and take a firm stand there where he feels solid ground. And such a student is not depressed.

[b] Structure and the new educational methods

Our second guideline is related to dialogue and small-group living in the seminary. Both are highly moral activities which require someone who is able to take the responsibility. If it is true that a discussion can unite as well as separate, and that a small group can be task-oriented as well as self-centred, we are involved in very sensitive areas of life which cannot be left to the process of trial and error. If nobody accepts this responsibility, emotions, ideas and plans will be like water which is not guided by a riverbed but splashes in all directions destroying land instead of irrigating it. He who accepts responsibility will be able to provide creative channels through which life can become purposive. Therefore our guideline here is that such sensitive processes as dialogue and group living require a well-defined responsibility in order to be effective.

This responsibility usually means that some form of leadership has to exist by which structure can be brought to dialogue and group processes. Let me mention different ways in which this leadership can function.

[a] Good leadership can prevent group processes from becoming amateur forms of group therapy. The expression of love and hate, anger and frustration, hostility and erotic desires, without special control, careful supervision and well-defined goals is dangerous and tends to harm people more than help them.

[b] Good leadership can foster at times of crisis the right atmosphere to discuss certain existential issues. Such a discussion can have a temporary value. When the leader is not just an equal participant, but represents more than an individual opinion, he can make it clear to the students that they are on safe ground and they are protected against dangerous traps.

[c] Good leadership keeps the communication in a group free and open. Nobody can be forced to enter a discussion if he does not want it. Many people just don't have anything to say or are not ready to say it. And subtle pressure to participate in a dialogue can take away the freedom of people to determine their own degree of intimacy.

Considering these aspects of good leadership it seems that the essential idea is that discussions and group living can only bring people closer together if they are already together in some way. Leadership means the representation of some level of community within which these processes can take place in a creative way. The leader's authority can be seen as an expression of the authority which belongs to the community in the first place. The task of a leader, therefore, can be seen as safeguarding the boundaries of the community and judging which ideas, feelings and actions can be handled within these boundaries and which not. And people will feel much freer to express themselves when they know that they will be warned when they trespass.

Therefore, good leadership offers an antidepressive regime by bringing the loaded question into the safe context of a community. And this brings us to our conclusion which finally allows us to ask what a religious community can be.

The Religious Community

After these 'therapeutic' considerations in which structure was the key word, we finally had to bring in the term community. Perhaps this is the most widely used term in recent discussions about religious life evoking feelings of great excitement as well as feelings of utter boredom. Up to this point we have tried to avoid this word in order to take a more critical look at the underlying dynamics. But by way of conclusion we need to bring this big word back to our attention and ask ourselves what it means in the context of the problem of seminary depression.

Religious community is *ecclesia*, which means called out of the land of slavery to the free land. It is constantly moving away from the status quo, searching for what is beyond the here and now. As soon as the community becomes sedentary, it is tempted to lose its faith and worship the house-gods instead of the one true God who is leading it in a pillar of fire.

If we speak about vocation we have to ask first of all if the community has a vocation that means experiencing itself as being called out of Egypt, the land of depression, to a new as yet undiscovered country. It seems that some communities have lost their élan and have become so enchanted by the beautiful oasis which they found on their way that they settled for that and forgot their real call.

I think that the vocation of the individual seminarian can be seen as a participation in the vocation of the community. When many students leave the seminary these days, this might very well be due to the fact that they have not been able to find the vocation in which they can participate. Instead they found a group of people very preoccupied with internal conflicts, wrapped up in small, insignificant debates about rituals, rules and authorities, and remarkably blind to the fact that most of their energy is spoiled by trivia while the world is on the verge of committing suicide. These self-centred communities tend to throw the student back on himself and encourage him to be very reflective, suggesting that vocation is an internal inspiration which cannot be discovered unless through endless self-scrutiny. This causes the seminarian to take himself much too seriously and to ask his superiors to pay constant attention to his most individual needs and desires. I think that the problem usually is not with the students who want to give their best, nor with the faculty who are willing to do anything for their students, but with the community at large, which has lost its most basic conviction that its existence is mandatory because it is called to fulfil a task nobody else will fulfil.

There is no lack of generosity. There is so much of it that everyone who can mobilize it and channel it can make mountains move and oceans hold their waves. I am convinced that a community which feels called to do a most difficult task, which asks for great sacrifices and great self-denial in order to do the work of God which is obvious and self-evident, will have no problems at all in finding people who want to join in the challenging enterprise. He who promises hard work, long hours, and much sacrifice will attract the strong and generous but he who promises protection, success and all the facilities of an affluent society will have to settle for the weak, the lazy and the spoiled. It is sad to say, but it is not always the weak and the lazy who leave our seminaries, but often the strong and the generous who had too much to give to do their best in an easy life.

The task of the religious community is to constantly move away out of the comfortable situation and to look for areas where only one who is willing to give his life wants to go. This can be everything: education, hospital work, mission work, etc. But as soon as any of these enterprises starts to become very profitable and successful we should know that this is a state of temptation and a challenge to cut the ties again, and to move on to new areas. And much of the depression we discovered in our diagnosis might be considered in the final analysis as a sign that the community is tempted to stop being *ecclesia* and to lose contact with the pillar of fire. A religious community can only survive when it stays in contact with this fire. It is the same fire which was the symbol of the new community on the day of Pentecost. Instead of huddling together and clinging to each other in fear, the apostles opened their doors, stepped into the world and went out in different directions. They knew that they were carried and supported by more than just the psychological experience of sympathy and friendship.

That is what Jesus indicated to the hard-headed Peter when He asked him three times: 'Do you love Me more than these others do?' Jesus meant *agape*, not *phileia*. It took Peter a while to understand the difference. But Jesus meant that only this Divine love, *agape*, would make it possible for him to fulfil his vocation. Because this vocation meant that he would not any longer put on his own belt and walk where he liked, but stretch out his hands and let somebody else put a belt around him, and take him where he would rather not go (John 21:18). Only by growing old would Peter be able to do this. The formation in the seminary is meant to allow this growth to the mature man who strengthened by the new love is able to understand that the cross is no longer a sign of depression but a sign of hope.

Intimacy and the Ministry

&

The Priest and His
Mental Health

6

If you were ever present at the admission of a severely disturbed patient to a mental hospital, you might have been surprised by some of the questions asked by the psychiatrist. Instead of asking: 'What is the problem?' or 'What is bothering you?' he sometimes says: 'Can you tell me what time it is, do you know what day it is, what month is this, what year is this?' Then he inquires: 'What is the name of this town and what country are we in?' And finally he asks: 'What is your name, who are your friends, and what job do you have?'

Why does a doctor ask all these obvious questions? He wants to know if the patient knows: when he is, where he is, and who he is. Because basic to man's mental health is that he is oriented in time, place, and person, or – to say the same – that man is realistically aware of himself.

But what is most basic to our mental health is also crucial in all levels of our behaviour. The painful and difficult problems in our life are always related to essentials. We cannot exist without being loved, but nevertheless to love and to be loved remains our main concern through life. In the same way, being oriented in time, place, and person is at the root of our mental health. As we grow up and are confronted with new bits of reality every day of our life, this remains a constant challenge, especially for those whose world is in the midst of turmoil, subjected to severe reevaluation and extreme self-criticism. That is our world, and perhaps especially the world of the priest. The question: 'When, where and who am I?' might after all not be easy to answer when asked by the priest in the modern world. Suddenly and painfully confronted with new and confusing realities, he might lose his orientation. And this means that his mental health is threatened.

Therefore, I will discuss the mental health of the priest in the world in terms of healthy timing, healthy spacing, and healthy self-understanding, and show how problems in these three areas can become a source of mental suffering for the priest in the modern world.

I. HEALTHY TIMING

Healthy timing is perhaps one of the most obvious and nevertheless least understood problems for priests. Let us have a look at two forms of timing: long-range timing and short-term timing.

Long-range timing refers to the way a priest uses his days, weeks, and months in the perspective of an effective life plan. I don't think that it is an exaggeration to say that many newly ordained priests leave the seminary with great ambitions, high aspirations and often zealous expectations. The excited new priest tends to jump into his pastoral activities as a true follower of Pelagius. He very soon can become the victim of what by distant observers has been called 'A redemption complex'. He is almost omnipresent, as far as his territory goes. No Bible group, no P.T.A. meeting, no Boy Scouts practice, Holy Name gathering, social, financial or pious meeting exists without his being there. He talks with almost everyone who wants to talk with him, gives advice to troubled parishioners, counsels couples, teaches classes to grade, trade and high school, and is constantly available for everybody's needs, except perhaps his own. He seldom refuses an invitation, seldom says no, and seldom withdraws to his private room. And he receives his rewards. He is popular, well-liked by his parishioners. They call him nice, kind, and under-standing, and say: 'This man is really giving himself for his people. He at least understands what is going on. He is different from the old pastor. This young man is available for us, all the time.' Indeed, all the time. With a certain pride he tells his col-leagues that he hardly gets more than five hours sleep a night, that he never has an opportunity to read a book except his breviary, that he does not even have an hour free to play a game of golf.

Well, you know what this is: The redemption complex in full bloom. But how long does it last? Two, four or five years, per-haps, then things start to look different. He has not been able to change the world around him as he had hoped, people are not so much different from the way they were during his first year. The same old problems keep coming up, but they don't look so exciting anymore. No new books or ideas have entered his room. Then, slowly, but sometimes very pervasively, a feeling of dullness and boredom can creep in and the question comes up: 'What am I doing after all? Nothing is really changing and I am getting tired of activities, people, and myself.'

Fatigue – physical, because of lack of sleep; mental, because of lack of motivation; and spiritual, because of lack of inspira-tion – takes over and leads to neutral resignation, growing irri-tation, or even to eroding depression.

We can call this unhealthy long-range timing. The so-popular, inspiring, creative priest has become, in a few years, an irritated, empty, routine, tired man, who keeps repeating to himself, if not on the pulpit, that since Jesus Christ nothing really has changed, and that there is nothing new under the sun. And many priests who were the hope of the diocese or the star of the order become bitter and disappointed men; some clinging to the priesthood to keep some sort of a home, others leaving it in the hope of starting a new life somewhere else.

But this is still somewhat exceptional. Much more common is the unhealthy short-term timing. Short-term timing refers to the way a priest uses his hours during one day. It seems to me that it is extremely important that the priest has a time to work and a time to relax. There are ways of living in which it is difficult to say whether a person is creating or recreating. A priest who lives in the rectory all day and is surrounded by his colleagues, in a way, is always in his office. People can call him every hour of the day and he is never completely outside the work atmosphere. On the other hand, he can rest at very unusual hours and is always also in his home where he eats, sleeps, plays and prays. So there is very little definition of time. This can result in a feeling of being always busy day and night, without really either working hard or resting well. He has some scheduled activities, but otherwise his work is pretty well at random. The priest is never very certain about what he will be doing during the next hours. To a man with a high sense of duty, this can become extremely frustrating. The lack of gratification can result in a feeling of: 'I did not do enough' and impels him to do more in his free hours, with the effect that his disappointment with himself only increases.

When the distinctions between day and night, work and play, duty and hobby, become fuzzy, life loses its rhythm and becomes poorly defined. Such 'unhealthy living' may kill inspiration and creativity by making a man the victim rather than the organizer of his time. He is always on the go and seldom stops to reflect on the meaning and effectiveness of his busy life. And sometimes it seems that he is afraid to stand still and think, afraid to discover that being busy and tired is quite something else from being useful.

It is clear that this problem is closely related to celibacy. A priest never leaves home to go to work and never comes back after having fulfilled his daily task, to find someone who helps him take some distance. He is always at home and never at home; he is always at work and never at work, and he wears his uniform always without any distinction of time or kind of activity. This unhealthy short-term timing also can soon lead to fatigue as a constant complaint and to boredom as a constant mood.

In short, healthy timing is essential for the physical, mental and spiritual health of the priest, not only in terms of the long-range effectiveness in his life as a priest, but also in terms of his creativity and inspiration in daily life.

2. HEALTHY SPACING

Besides a healthy use of time, a healthy use of place is of great importance for the mental health of the priest. We can speak about healthy spacing. Seminarians, diocesan and religious priests mostly live in houses where they share all the various aspects of their lives under one roof. One of the critical problems of the Catholic seminary today is called its 'total institutionalization'. This means that every level of living of the student – his religious formation, his academic training, his social life and his physical education – are all institutionalized and under the same roof, the same rule, and the same authority. The one very defined milieu pervades and covers all the levels of the life of the student.

And this is not only true of the seminary, but in many ways also of the religious community life and of the rectory life. It seems that there is only one organization which can compete with the Catholic church in terms of total institutionalization, and that is the military.

The priest or seminarian often finds himself in a situation which is experienced as suffocating. If he eats or drinks, plays or prays, sleeps or stays up at night, studies or day dreams, goes to a movie or to a play, all his activities are directly or indirectly under the same authority. He is enclosed.

One of the reasons why a man in the business or academic world is often able to tolerate considerable frustration is exactly related to the fact that he does not find his demanding boss back in his private home, that in his interracial committee he can be leader; that if he goes on a vacation with his wife and children he has authority and responsibility which is different from his authority and responsibility in his profession; that when he goes to the country club he can temporarily forget his conflict with his wife and his problems with his kids. In other words, there are different roofs under which he lives: his home, his office, his cottage, his country club, his church, all representing different realities of life with different authorities and responsibilities. They indicate different levels of living, not completely separated, but distinct enough to be able to function as a mechanism to prevent, compensate, or take away many strains and pressures of daily life. If your superior is bugging you, you at least don't have to face him all day. If you always have to smile and be nice as a tourist guide, you at least can be mad and angry at home for a while. If you cannot say what you think about your secretary in your office, you at least have a chance to let your steam off with your friends in the bar. Different places and different spaces. That can create a healthy balance.

The seminarian or priest often lacks this variation. Whatever he thinks, feels, does, says or writes is finally under the critical eye of the same authority or string of authorities. A parish pastor not only expects his assistant to do responsible professional work between 8 and 5, he also wants him to play bridge with him once a week, to socialize with some of his friends, to join him for a dinner party and perhaps even play golf with him. But he also may expect him not to drink too much beer, not to talk with prostitutes on the street, not to wear a tie, not to buy a Thunderbird, and not to receive girls in his room. This is what might be called spiritual suffocation and causes many seminarians and priests to feel caught in a web of unclear relations from which they cannot free themselves without tearing loose. Leaving the priesthood can then become a way to get some fresh air.

Closely related to healthy spacing is the problem of authority vs. responsibility. The question is: 'To what extent are we boss under our own roof?' First of all, in the Catholic church we are very quick to delegate responsibility but very slow to delegate authority. Many sermons, lectures, and talks are aimed at convincing us of the tremendous responsibility of the priest in the modern world. But the authority which belongs to this responsibility is not always a part of the package. A priest is responsible for the good atmosphere in the house, but he cannot always change the rules; responsible for a meaningful liturgy, but he cannot experiment very much; responsible for good teaching, but he has to follow the prescribed sequence of subjects, and especially responsible for good advice, but he does not feel free to give his own opinion because he has to represent someone else's authority instead of his own. In reality, this means that in a setting of total institutionalization every sphere of life is controlled from one central point. This has its advantages. After all, the general of an army cannot win a war if he has only partial command over his troops or if that command only lasts from 8 in the morning until 5 in the evening. The question for a priest, however, is whether he is really at war.

But there is another perhaps more complicated problem. That is the problem of the shadow government. Those who have authority do not always know how much they really have. Often they suffer from lack of clarity. The superior of a house does not know how far he can go because a bishop is watching him somewhere; the bishop does not know how far he can go because the apostolic delegate is looking over his shoulder, and the apostolic delegate is not sure exactly what Rome thinks. The problem is not that some have more authority than others, but that there is no clarity and that the further one gets from the problem the thicker the clouds become. Perhaps a lot of fear and anxiety about authority is not so much related to power but to the cloudiness of power, which leaves the responsible people always hanging shadowy in the air. Nobody knows who is really saying what and the further away from home the vaguer and the more anonymous people become. This is what I mean by the shadow government, which causes this constant referral to eternity, where all lines melt together in a quasi-sacred mystery that cannot be touched.

In short, healthy spacing not only refers to healthy defining of places and rooms, but also, connected with that, to healthy clarification of responsibilities and authority which belong to the different roofs under which we live.

3. HEALTHY SELF-UNDERSTANDING

But after all this, we still have not arrived at the core of the matter. More fundamental than healthy timing and healthy spacing is healthy self-understanding. In this tumbling and changing world the priest is faced with the most central question: 'Who am I?' The rapidly diminishing number of vocations to the priesthood all over the world is dramatically showing that along with the whole church, the priest has entered into an identity crisis. He is asking himself: 'Who am I and what can I do?'

In discussing the priest's reality orientation in terms of person, we will make a distinction between his individual and his professional identity.

[a] If someone's individual identity crisis concerns the basic levels of his personality he suffers from a severe pathology. Deep depression, obsessive compulsive action, and different forms of psychotic behaviour indicate that psychiatric help and sometimes hospitalization are needed. Although perhaps few priests suffer from these severe forms of identity confusion, this basic problem is, in some degree, the problem of every man – but perhaps more of every priest.

How does the priest see himself in his relationship with his fellow man? How does he relate privacy to fellowship, intimacy to social intercourse? Essentially, human existence is 'being together'. I am not alone in the world but I share this world with others. To be able to live a healthy life in this world which judges me and asks me to play a role according to my physical identity, two things are necessary. First, that I must have my own inner privacy where I can hide from the face of the challenging world; and secondly, I must establish a hierarchy of relationships with this same world. In the inner circle of my life I find him or her who is closest to me. Around this circle of intimacy I find the circle of family and dear friends. Then, at a somewhat larger distance, I locate relatives, and acquaintances and, even further away, the associates in business and work. Finally, I am aware of the vast circle of people that I don't know by name but who in some vague way also belong to this world, which I can call *my* world. Thus, I am surrounded by expanding circles on the threshold of which I station guards, who carefully check whom they allow to enter into a closer intimacy with me. I don't say to the bus driver what I can say to my colleagues. I don't say to my friends what I can say to my parents. But there is a place where nobody can enter, where I am completely by myself, where I develop my own most inner privacy. This is the place where I can meet God, who by His incarnation has thrown off his otherness. The possibility for a man to hide from the face of the world is a condition for the formation of any community. A man who does not have privacy cannot be a part of a community.

It is exactly here that the priest has problems. Very often he has lost his private life, where he can be with himself; nor has he a hierarchy of relationships with guards on the thresholds. Being friendly to everybody, he very often has no friends for himself. Always consulting and giving advice, he often has nobody to go to with his own pains and problems. Not finding a real intimate home in his house or rectory, he often rambles through the parish to find people who give him some sense of belonging and some sense of a home. The priest, who is pleading for friends, needs his parishioners more than they need him. Looking for acceptance, he tends to cling to his counsellees, and depend on his faithful. If he has not found a personal form of intimacy where he can be happy, his parishioners become his needs. He spends long hours with them, more to fulfil his own desires than theirs. In this way he tends to lose the hierarchy of relationships, never feels safe, is always on the alert, and finally finds himself terribly misunderstood and lonely.

The paradox is that he who has been taught to love everyone, in reality finds himself without any friends; that he who trained himself in mental prayer often is not able to be alone with himself. Having opened himself to every outsider, there is no room left for the insider. The walls of the intimate enclosure of his privacy crumble and there is no place left to be with himself. The priest who has given away so much of himself creates an inexhaustible need to be constantly with others in order to feel that he is a whole person.

And here the priest is in a crisis situation. Without a spiritual life and a good friend he is like a sounding brass or a tinkling cymbal. This might impress you as an old-fashioned sermon, unless you realize that the question underneath is: 'Who guides him who has to guide his people?' No psychotherapist will feel competent to help people if he himself is not willing to constantly reevaluate his own mental health with professional help. But which priest has a spiritual director who helps him to find his way through the complexities of his and others' spiritual lives? There are hundreds of priests who are able theologians, good preachers, excellent organizers, brilliant writers, highly competent sociologists, psychologists, mathematicians and philosophers; but how many are there who can help their fellowmen and especially, their fellow priests, in their most individual spiritual needs? Those seem to be as seldom as white crows. Perhaps one of the most urgent questions remains: 'Who is the pastor for the priest?'

[b] This brings us to our final and perhaps most specific concern, the professional identity of the priest. Healthy self-understanding not only means a healthy understanding of yourself as an individual in the world, but also a healthy understanding of yourself as a professional man.

The first and most obvious question seems to be: Do we actually have a profession? We live in a society which is characterized by a rapidly growing professionalization. We see a growing number of professionally trained people: doctors, psychiatrists, psychologists, social workers, lawyers, judges, architects, engineers, and nearly every year new professions seem to create themselves. In the psychiatric field we now speak about music therapists, group-therapists, occupational therapists, etc. Everyone has his own speciality, with his own training and his own place in the team of the professions. Where does this leave the priest? What is his speciality? What is his own unique contribution? Is it not true that many priests feel extremely frustrated because they feel that they know a little bit of everything but are not really good in anything? Many feel that they are amateur counsellors, amateur social workers, amateur psychologists, amateur group leaders and amateur teachers, but when and where are they really pros? And it is not surprising that many priests are very uncomfortable in a professional milieu, and, in spite of their four or five years of post-graduate training, feel more at ease with the so-called 'simple people'.

Priests have pretty good reasons to feel this way. A doctor, after four years of theoretical training, needs at least two years of internship under close supervision before he is allowed to practice by himself. A psychologist cannot start his independent work before at least two years of practical training in a very controlled supervisory setting. A social worker does not earn his title without many years of very strict guidance in his professional field. But what about a priest? Most priests study four years of theology and then jump right into the pastoral work without any internship whatsoever. And of those who have a pastoral year only very few receive the needed supervision to make their experience in practice a real learning experience. Who supervised their sermons carefully? Who critically studied and discussed their pastoral conversations? Who helped them to express in the liturgy something meaningful through their hands, voice and eyes? And especially, who helped them to consider the relevance of their knowledge and information – stored up during four years of theory – for their very specific relationship with the confused teenager, the searching college student, the doubtful husband, the despairing father or the depressed widow? Who helped them to ask if their pastoral expectations are realistic or if their desires and needs are tolerable? Who taught them to make intelligent choices and accept possible failures? Who explored with them their limitations, and who taught them to handle the complicated authority problems in relationships with superiors as well as with parishioners? Who inspired them to do more study and research in their own field, and who finally guided them in the integration of new experience? In short, who made them real professionals?

The sociologist, Osmund Schreuder, writes: 'The crisis in regard to the priesthood in our time seems to be related to the professional underdevelopment of this occupation.'[1] If this is true, we face a mental health problem because a man who permanently doubts his own competence can hardly be considered mentally healthy.

A second question is: Even if our work is professional, is it a rewarding profession? A professional man who works hard and is creative, receives his rewards. People tell him how they appreciate his work. They praise him, give him a higher salary, and offer him a promotion. And the visible and tangible rewards make him appreciate his profession more. What about the priest? Many priests seem to experience their work as simply filling a position which happened to be open. They are not there because of the specific professional skill which they can apply to that specific situation but they are there because no other priest was there for the job. And once in the job, nobody really cares what he does. As long as he doesn't do stupid things, does not write letters to the editor and does not generally disrupt the existing order, he doesn't hear anything. The reward of the quiet priest is silence from above.

Few religious authorities praise their men. They expect them to do their job and not to ask for a 'thank you'. Perhaps many priests have even denied themselves the desire to be praised, thanked, paid and appreciated. Some distorted view on obedience seems to forbid a desire for gratification and satisfaction. It is amazing to see how few priests can accept a real compliment. They are not used to it and feel somewhat embarrassed, as if they are not allowed to be complimented. But when all the gratification you get out of your study is your grades at the end of

[1] Osmund Schreuder, 'Het professioneel karakter van het geestelijk ambt' (*Dekker en van de Vegt*, Nijmegen 1964), p. 7.

the semester, you are less mentally healthy than when you enjoy your study daily and have a good grade on top of that. Daily life in the latter case, is fun. In the former case, you have a lot of pain for the sake of a little gratification. If a priest does not enjoy his daily pastoral work and is only hoping for God's grade at the end of his life, his mental health is in danger. And so is his most important task of bringing life and happiness to his fellow man.

There is one form of gratification which is most absent in the daily life of the parish priest, and that is the gratification of his professional theological discipline. Every professional man knows that his task is not only to keep informed in his field, but also to offer a creative contribution to it. The doctor and psychologist know that while working with people they are helping them best when at the same time they are looking for new insights for the sake of their discipline. A doctor who sees hundreds of allergic patients might, by a systematic way of treating them, not only serve his patients but also his science.

Are there pastors who realize that the people they are working with every day form one of the main sources for their theological understanding? Since God became man, man became the main source for the understanding of God. The parish is just as much a field of research for the priest as the hospital is for the doctor. Perhaps nobody made us so much aware of the need of this empirical theology as the Protestant mental-hospital chaplain, Anton Boisen, who wrote: 'Just as no historian worthy of the name is content to accept on authority the simplified statement of some other historian regarding the problem under investigation, so I have sought to begin, not with ready made formulations contained in books, but with the living human documents and with actual social conditions in all their complexity.'[2]

2 Anton Boisen, *The Exploration of the Inner World* (Harper & Brothers: 1962), p. 185.

The priest is confronted every day with living human documents, and if he is able to read and understand them and make them a constant source for his theological reflection, his life can always be new, surprising, inspiring and creative. There is no human problem, human conflict, human happiness, or human joy, which cannot lead to a deeper understanding of God's work with man.

In this way his profession asks him to remain responsible for God, to keep God alive always changing and always the same, as man himself. And it is here that the priest can find himself at the heart of his profession.

Healthy self-understanding. This was our last and main concern. Healthy understanding of our own individual self realistically related to the other on the basis of a sound spiritual life and a sense for intimacy, and healthy understanding of our professional self, which gives us a humble, gratifying, and scholarly place in the team of the helping professions.

This brings us to the end of this orientation session. Is the priest oriented in time, place and person? Does he know when he is, where he is and who he is? Our roaring days are threatening his balance, balance between private and public life, between places to be reserved and places to be shared, between contemplation and action, between study and work. This threat creates anxiety. And this hurts. But if the wounds are understood, it might very well be a constructive anxiety. Then an honest diagnosis serves a good prognosis.

Training for Campus Ministry

During the Second World War, many army chaplains, Protestant and Catholic, were faced with a very difficult question: How to be a pastor without a church? In the field there is no pulpit to speak from, no altar to stand behind, no bible class to direct, no discussion group to lead. Many felt like carpenters who had lost their tools. They had to ask themselves, 'Can I do something without anything but myself? Can I be a priest without a collar, a book, or a chalice?' In this emergency situation, thousands of men ran to the quickly organized seminars to get some basic training in this new field work.

Perhaps our University campuses today are like the battle-fields of the Second World War. The familiar channels through which we could function and reach thousands of students are leaking or completely broken down. Religious bulletins, processions, rosaries and holy hours are strange memories that evoke a smile. Chapels have become less popular places to visit. Masses and other celebrations only attract a small section of the campus population. Bible clubs, discussion groups, and retreats are liked, perhaps by many, but we wonder for how long. And as time goes on we feel ourselves victims of a religious strip tease in which students are insisting we remove one vestment of office after another, as if to say: 'We want to see you naked, and then we will see what you are worth.'

159

In short: We cannot rely on old channels and prepared roads, but we are thrown back on our most personal resources and faced with a great deal of anxiety. To use the image of Erwin Goodenough: The curtains through which we communicated with the divine, are torn down and we wonder if we can live without them.[1]

In the middle of this confusion we ask for training. But can we speak about training if we are not clear about its object? What does it mean to be a campus minister? If we are able to delineate the role of the campus minister, we also will be able to lay bare the main areas for training. Therefore, I propose first to raise two questions closely related to one another.

1 How can the priest be an efficient and skilful pastor in a campus community?
2 How can he remain a whole and integrated man in a milieu which is constantly changing and by its own nature repeatedly challenging his own commitment?

You will probably realize that the second question is much more important than the first, however seldom asked. But let us start where the question is asked and then break through to the level where it hurts. Then, finally, we are free to ask the last question.

3 What is the best way to prepare a man for this special ministerial task?

1 Erwin R. Goodenough, *The Psychology of Religious Experiences* (Basic Books: 1965).

I. THE EFFICIENT AND SKILFUL CAMPUS MINISTER

Although the faculty and other personnel related to the university also ask for his attention, the main pastoral concern of the campus minister is the student. We will focus on the pastoral care for the student.

For most students, the patterns of life were pretty clear and well-defined during their high-school years. Home and school were closely related and many customs, practices, rules, and regulations, although often criticized in their particular form, were seldom questioned on a basic level. There were many problems, but problems could be solved. There were many questions, but every question had an answer. There were many stupid teachers, but the smart ones knew what they were talking about.

But at college things became different. Being away from home, without strong anchors in the family tradition, and without a clear goal on the horizon, the student starts drifting. Familiar answers do not work anymore, long cherished beliefs lose their obviousness, and carefully built structures crumble, sometimes suddenly, sometimes gradually. And in this new milieu where science sets the tone, where research is the main approach and hypothesis the main model, certainty becomes the most suspected attitude and the question mark the most respected symbol. But asking questions is a fearful thing. The answer might be No. Do I have anything to hope for in my future? Yes or No? Is love a real human possibility? Yes or No? Is there anybody who cares for anybody except himself? Yes or No? And finally: Is life worth living? Yes or No? Asking these questions is a dangerous thing to do. Many may prefer to stay away from them and do their daily business because it seems much safer to hold to 'the way they think and act at home' than to rock the boat in such a stormy sea. But if the student used to the microscope, familiar with Skinner boxes and proud of his

161

computer techniques, avoids asking these questions about the core values which give meaning to any tool at all, he takes the risk of becoming an unhappy genius, a man who knows everything except why he lives.

It is in this milieu that the campus priest has to be a pastor. What should he be able to offer to the student? I propose to discuss this under three titles: *a climate, a word, a home.*

I. A climate

Perhaps the real desire of many students is not primarily to find an answer to the deep and often painful questions related to the meaning of being but to find a climate in which he is allowed to ask these questions without fear. Most amazing about many Christian milieux is the great taboo on asking questions. You know how questions about the divinity of Christ, the virginity of Mary, the priesthood of women, the advisability of abortion, and even about a good selection process for bishops might not be just food for an interesting discussion but would spoil many meals in a rectory. These questions seem to be more than interesting; they are dangerous and explosive. Questioning the morality of war, the value of academic progress, the meaning of monogamy may cause people to throw stones through your windows because all these questions suggest that the safe little playpen we have set up for ourselves might be nothing more than a subtle form of self-deception. But if we are so afraid to face a question which comes from without, how much more threatening will the question be which comes from within? Is it really worth eating and drinking, studying and fighting, living and being? We know that the most common form of mental suffering on campuses today is depression. Depression is caused by questions which cannot be asked and which are swallowed and inverted into the experience of deep guilt. The question, 'Why do I live?' is turned into a castigating self-doubt, 'Is it worthwhile to live?'

Can the priest tolerate this question? Can he offer a climate in which the most basic doubts can be expressed without fear, where the most sacred realities can be unveiled without creating the need to defend, where despair can be allowed to be despair without the need to fill the threatening holes? Can he accept agnosticism? That is, can he accept the fact that we do not know the reality in which we live? A man who lives in a scientific milieu has to learn to be happy with a little bit of knowledge. Goodenough states: 'The true agnostic is not interested in whether man can ever "know" the truth as a whole; what he wants is to find out a little more than he knows now.'[2]

If Christianity is not a panacea for every doubt, ignorance, and impotence, it might create the possibility of being an agnostic without being afraid, of being happy without a cure-all and safe without a playpen. Gordon Allport considers as one of the attributes of a mature religion *its heuristic character*. He writes, 'A heuristic belief is one that is held tentatively until it can be confirmed, or until it helps us discover a more valid belief.'[3] If this characteristic can develop anywhere, it should on a college campus. But what is needed is a climate to allow searching without fear, and questioning without shame. The first demand of a question is not to be answered but to be accepted. Then the problem of faith can become the mystery of faith and the problem of God, the mystery of God. As long as the priest considers atheism as the only alternative for orthodoxy and unbelief as the only alternative for dogma, every question put to him will be felt as a threat and every doubt as an attack calling for defence. But his faith tells him that growth can only take place

[2] *ibid.*, p. 182.
[3] Gordon Allport, *The Individual and His Religion* (Macmillan), p. 72.

when belief and unbelief, doubt and faith, hope and despair can exist together. It is only slowly that a student is willing to realize this, and he will never be able to do it unless there is someone to offer him a fearless climate.

2. A word

Many have already said, since St Paul, that faith comes from hearing, and that the word of God is all we have to give. But few were wise enough, as was St Paul, to realize that not every word is for everyone, that some need milk and others solid food. Diagnosis has been one of the weakest qualities in the pastoral field. What doctor would give all his pills to all his patients? What psychologist would administer all his tests to all his clients? What counsellor would give all his advice to all his counsellees? Their training is geared to diagnosis, based on the insight that not everything is good for everyone, and that help only can be given on the basis of the clinical understanding of the unique needs of our fellow man. But it is sad to see that so much pastoral activity is based on the supposition that all the good words are good for everyone. And often the pastor behaves like a poor salesman who wants to sell the whole church as a package at once to everyone he happens to meet.

Much pastoral phoniness is related to the inability to be clinical in pastoral contact and pastoral conversation. Not everyone needs encouragement, not everyone asks for correction, not everyone is ready to be invited to prayer or to hear the name of God. Some ask for silence, some for a single word, some need instruction, some just understanding, some want a smile, some a severe hand, some need support, and some need to be left alone. Perhaps much of today's anti-clericalism on campuses is related to the insensitivity of men whose vocation is to care for the most individual need. If anybody is aware of his own

individuality and unique needs, it is the student who is studying to find *his* place in *his* world. The fact that many prefer a
psychologist to a priest is less related to the different ideas they
have to offer than it is to the fact that the one thinks diagnosti-
cally and clinically and the other often globally and generally.
And therefore, the campus minister should be able to offer a
word which is an honest response to the unique and highly
individual needs of the students.

3. A home

The third and perhaps most difficult thing to offer is a home
where some degree of intimacy can be experienced. In our modern highly demanding, and competitive university, which is
everything but a Schola – a place to be free – many students
suffer from an intense feeling of loneliness. They are very self-
conscious, constantly on their watchtower to register carefully
all the movements of their surroundings, hyper-alert to the reactions of their teachers and fellow students. They have their
antennas out to pick up all those signs which can suggest the
way to good grades, good letters of recommendation, good grad
schools, and good jobs. For many, it has become a matter of life
and death because they know that if you can't carry books,
there will be little else than rifles to carry. Many experience
some sense of self-contempt and have lost the ability to be with
themselves. In this highly stress-filled situation, intimacy has
become nearly impossible for many students. And although in
this searching time of life there is a heightened desire for
warmth, tenderness, and disarmed relaxation, for many students their roommate is more a stranger than a buddy, their
classmates more rivals than friends, their teachers more authorities than guides. This craving for intimacy is perhaps one of
the most central concerns for the campus minister. How can

he, in some way, somewhat satisfy this nearly inexhaustible need?

The answer is obvious but at the same time immense. It is the creation of a community where the student can experience some sense of belonging. If the years of free search are not surrounded by some form of intimacy and lived in some form of community, the search may be bitter instead of mild, narrow-minded instead of mature, cold and calculated instead of open and receptive.

There are many ways in which we have tried and do try to form these communities: discussion groups, weekends, retreats or advances, many forms of celebration and most of all the Eucharist. Crucial to all these forms seems to be the creation of a healthy balance between closeness and distance. The campus minister can be the guardian of this very subtle balance. This is very difficult because the need for intimacy can be so strong that it finds expression in a suffocating embrace. Different forms of intense mutual confession, sharing of feelings, and repeated physical contact may seem a good sign on a campus which counts so many alienated students but, in fact, can create cliques instead of community, stickiness instead of freedom, and even fear instead of love. In this desire to experience some oneness, students might cling to each other instead of freely communicating. And if the campus minister sees a growing interest in Pentecostalism, cursillos, group-dynamics, and very informal liturgies, he should not only ask himself to what extent do these new groups satisfy obvious present needs, but also to what extent will they offer in the long run the freedom and maturity the student is looking for.

In the many new experiments in liturgy on campus, the balance between closeness and distance seems to be essential for the maturity of the Christian. A good liturgy is a liturgy with full participation without a pressure to participate, a liturgy with free expression and dialogue without an urge to be too personal, a liturgy where man is free to move in closer or to take more distance without feeling that he is offending people, and a liturgy where physical contact is real but does not break through the symbolic boundaries. I don't think there will ever be a single good liturgy. The personality of the minister, the nature of the students, and the climate of the place ask for many different forms. But much more important than the particular format, canon, language, or gesture is the careful balance between closeness and distance which allows the Christian community to be intimate *and* open, to be personal *and* hospitable, to receive the daily core-group as well as the occasional visitors, to be nurturing as well as apostolic.

The problem of intimacy is very often experienced as the core problem of the emotional life of the young adult. His relationships with female as well as male friends often can be clouded by painful anxieties. Closeness is desirable as well as fearful, and it asks for a careful guide to find a vital balance which can lead to a life in which one can be committed and open-minded at the same time.

Summarizing the special skills which can make the campus minister an efficient and skilful pastor we might say: He should offer a climate, in which the student can raise basic questions without fear, a word which is an honest response to his individual needs, and a home where he can experience intimacy with a vital balance between closeness and distance.

2. THE SPIRITUALITY OF THE CAMPUS MINISTER

But all we have said until this moment seems rather trivial and superficial if we consider it just in terms of skills for efficient ministry. I hope you have already become aware of the fact that, all the way through, the minister himself is involved most personally, most individually, and often most painfully. If our real concern is the making of the 'whole man', 'the mature Christian', we cannot avoid the question: How can the minister himself become and remain a whole and integrated man in a community which is constantly changing and by its own nature constantly challenging his commitment?

In many ways the campus community is the most demanding and tiring place for a minister to work. Every four years his parish is completely de-and-repopulated. Each time he is once again faced with a new wave of searching, questioning, critical men and women who usually have mixed feelings when they are invited to contact the priest. Over and over again, he is asked to respond to the powerful feelings of doubt, aggression and loneliness and to act as guide in the intensive struggle for self-discovery and meaning in life. This means a constant request for honesty, authenticity, openness, and a nearly bottomless availability. And when he finally, often after a long time, has received confidence and established some community, he will find that graduation is often the end of it all. Students go away and keep going away. The minister stays. Except for some cards at Christmas, he does not hear very much any more and thanks are seldom expressed. He knows that students have to leave; he even knows that they should not become too attached to the school or to him and that an education to independence sometimes also includes a renunciation of thanks; but he also knows how much it hurts when people, in whom he has invested so much of his own self, leave him. How often can a man build with care and patience a personal relationship with people who will be running away so soon only to look back at their college years as a part of their necessary preparation for life? For the student, college is just a temporary phase; for the minister, it is a way of living. And finally, how much questioning can a man take? Can he allow people to ask him all the time: Why are you a priest? Why do you believe in God? Why do you pray? Can he allow himself to be flexible all the time and willing to shift gears, to incorporate new ideas, to scrutinize new criticism and to question again his basic convictions? But this is exactly what happens, when students ask questions because every question about the meaning of life is, at the same time, a question about the meaning of the ministry. The question, 'Why do I live?' is at the same time the question, 'Why are you a priest?' It is obvious that not only the student but also, and perhaps even more, the minister realizes that his own existence is at stake.

If it is true that a psychiatrist who works closely with people in conflicts has to watch his own emotional life very carefully, then this is even more the case for a priest who is in daily contact with ultimate questions of life and death. And just as X-rays can heal and hurt us, exposure to these questions can have good but also dangerous effects. It is not so surprising that campus ministers are often suffering from a considerable amount of stress and need serious pastoral care more than anybody else. Although every campus minister has his own personality and therefore asks for individual guidance, there seem to be some main problem areas which allow generalization. We will discuss these under three titles: silence, friendship, and insight.

I. Silence

A university is not only a place for intellectual pursuits but also for a good amount of intellectualization; not only a place for rational behaviour but also for elaborate rationalization. It is probably not only the most verbal place but also the most wordy and talkative place. And religion is not exempt from this phenomenon. The campus minister is exposed to a nearly unbelievable amount of words, arguments, ideas, concepts, and abstractions. How can he separate the sense from the nonsense, the holy words from the crazy ones? This problem is tremendous not only for the student but just as much for the minister who might fall into the temptation of adoring the products of man's consciousness, trying to catch even the divine in the net of his explicit awareness. He can become entangled in the ropes of his own sentences and unable to be moved by the great Power which is beyond his capacity to articulate.

And often the drama of the campus minister is that, trapped by the need to understand and to be understandable, he loses communication with the realities which – as he himself knows – are transcendent to his mind.

In this context the campus minister needs silence. Silence means rest, rest of body and mind, in which we become available for Him whose heart is greater than ours. That is very threatening; it is like giving up control over our actions and thoughts, allowing something creative to happen not by us but to us. Is it so amazing that we are so often tired and exhausted, trying to be masters of ourselves, wanting to grasp the ultimate meaning of our existence, struggling with our identity? Silence is that moment in which we not only stop the discussion with others but also the inner discussions with ourselves, in which we can breathe in freely and accept our identity as a gift. 'Not I live, but He lives in me.' It is in this silence that the spirit of God can pray in us and continue His creative work in us. We never will find God in students unless it is God within us who recognizes Himself in them. Without silence the Spirit will die in us and the creative energy of our life will float away and leave us alone, cold, and tired. Without silence we will lose our centre and become the victim of the many who constantly demand our attention.

2. Friendship

The second urgent need of the campus minister is friendship. Here we enter a very difficult area because it is the most sensitive one. But it has to be said that the campus minister who depends for friendship on students is in a very dangerous situation not just because of the fact that students will leave him after some years but more because friendship with students often paralyses the possibility of being their pastor. If the student community becomes the main source of the personal gratification and satisfaction of the priest, he easily becomes the victim of fluctuating sympathies and preferences and quickly loses his freedom. If he needs students to fill his emotional needs, he clings to them and is not able to maintain the distance which allows him to be different. And as soon as students experience his great desire to be intimate with them, to know details of their lives, to be invited to their parties and closely involved with their daily ups and downs, they lose the possibility of relating to him in a creative way.

The campus minister needs privacy, a home where he is not with students, and where he is free for himself. Just as no doctor could stay healthy if he would only see patients, and no psychiatrist could stay 'whole' if his private life and that of his clients would merge, so no campus minister will ever be able to function well over a long period of time if he would always be with students. It might seem that student problems are urgent and that they require immediate attention, but let us first of all ask ourselves, 'Do they really need us more than we need them?' The campus priest needs a home, a place where he can live with friends and have his own intimacy. Only then will he keep from drowning in the high and low waves of the fluctuating life of the university.

3. Insight

Besides silence and friendship, insight is one of the main constituents of the spirituality of the campus minister. By insight, we mean a sound perspective of the minister on the significance of his own priesthood. Although much suffering of today's priests derives from distorted emotions, we should not overlook the importance of a clear understanding of his task in the society of today. For many priests, it is not so much their needs for friendship and sympathy which limit their pastoral freedom as their theological outlook on their own existence. I just wonder how many guilt feelings of today's priests are related to their concept of God, their view of revelation, and their ideas about Jesus Christ and His church. If the campus minister thinks that *he* is responsible for the faith on campus, if he thinks that it is his task to bring as many students as possible to the sacraments, and if he thinks that the students' way to heaven is somehow related to their membership in the church, he can be sure that the campus is going to be his purgatory. Because not only can feelings influence thoughts, but thoughts can also create very deep and powerful emotions. In the mind of a priest for whom sacramentality is, in practice, identical with the reception of the sacraments, the growing unpopularity of confession and communion must create a considerable amount of anxiety and perhaps even self-reproach. For a man to whom the recognition of Jesus Christ as Saviour is the criterion of the fruitfulness of his priestly service, a modern college campus cannot do anything but cause deep-seated guilt feelings and much unhappiness. And if the satisfactiom of the campus minister is dependent on a growing conversion of students to his creed and belief, his work can hardly be more than suffocating.

Many priests are deeply concerned today. Faced with the rapid changes in church attitudes, they worry and even panic, sometimes to the point of declaring the days as wicked, the students as degenerate, and Christianity as burning its last candle. The question is: Are these concerns really pastoral concerns, or are they rather more signs of little faith? Perhaps we are too easily caught in the narrowness of our own theological insights. They can make us anxious instead of free, unbelievers instead of faithful, suspicious instead of trustful.

Can the priest dedicate himself fully to a so-called non-religious student without the hidden condition or hope for a future conformity to his belief? In an academic community, people are very sensitive to the slightest form of pressure – hypersensitive even. The most guarded freedom is the freedom of thought. Although we are committed to God-*Logos* who came to free us from the God-*Anangke*,[4] that is, to the Word of God who liberated us from the chains of our pressing needs, it is very difficult to allow God's Word to be completely free. Often we do not feel comfortable with a free moving Spirit and prefer a so-called realistic limitation and control. But the Truth is to set us free. A growing insight through study of the Word and a deepening understanding of our own task as witnesses of this Word can prevent us from being a victim of our own narrow-mindedness.

Silence, friendship, and insight are three aspects of the spirituality of the campus priest which seem important if he wants to become and remain a 'whole' and integrated man. If he wants to be a skilful and efficient minister who can offer a climate, a word, and a home for his students, he will soon find that without silence, friendship, and insight his fruitfulness will be very short-lived and temporary.

[4] Sigmund Freud: *The Future of an Illusion* (Doubleday Anchor Books. New York), p. 97.

3. TRAINING FOR THE CAMPUS MINISTRY

The two questions, how to be skilful and how to be whole, proved to be closely related. Together they not only delineate a picture of an ideal, perhaps utopian, campus minister, but they also circumscribe the main fields of training. This brings us to the final question: How should the training of the campus minister take place?

There are many settings in terms of time and place within which we can envision a training situation. We can think of a one-day-a-week programme extending over a whole year, of a series of intensive workshops, of a full-time summer programme, and ideally of a whole year of pastoral internship.

Programmes of this nature preferably should be planned on the campuses. If this is not possible other training fields, such as general and mental hospitals, educational centres, prisons, and industrial schools, could also be considered. But essential for every setting is that it offers supervised pastoral experience, that is, pastoral experience which through careful control becomes available for supervision by a competent and specially educated pastor.

Many future ministers are like people who have learned Spanish in school. They are able to read and perhaps even to write Spanish, but when they come to Mexico the best they can do is stutter. What they need is not just experience but also someone who constantly corrects their mistakes, makes them aware of their own idiosyncracies, and suggests new ways of expression according to the culture in which they find themselves. Experience without supervision can lead to the adaptation of poor patterns of behaviour which are very difficult to shake off. It can create narrow-mindedness because it tends to make us settle on the first thing which seems to work. Then the pastor becomes like the conceited foreigner who says: 'As long as they know what I am saying, who cares what mistakes I make?' But this just might be the reason that he always will remain a foreigner. Pastoral work is more than a language. It asks for our ability to touch the most sensitive areas of life, and requires us not only to understand the highly individual needs of the other but also the many complex responses of the self. Just as no surgeon would start operating after only having read books, no pastor should touch the soft and tender internal life of his fellow man with the great books and the powerful ideas he brought with him from the classroom. Let me give you an example:

A young deacon in Holland paid a house visit to a middle aged couple and explained to them in convincing terms that birth control was no longer any problem, that they had no reason to be concerned about their son who had stopped going to church, that celibacy would go out the window within a decade and that most devotions were perfect examples of magic. After his exposition the mother of the house thought for a while and then said meditatively: 'Nothing really has changed.' 'How do you mean?' asked the deacon. 'Well,' she mused, 'twenty years ago the priests told us what we should do and believe. Now, with the same intolerance, they tell us what we should not do and not believe. After all the problem is still the same.'

If this deacon wants to be sensitive to the real needs of his parishioner and if he wants to come to a better understanding of his own preoccupations he will be helped by supervised pastoral experience. Let us have a closer look now, first at the nature of the supervisory process and secondly at the kind of pastoral experience which can become available for supervision.

[a] The nature of the supervisory process

It is obvious that supervision is a very delicate art, which not only requires sensitivity, and a special understanding of the dynamics of the human relationships, but also demands careful preparation for the difficult task of individual professional guidance. It is sad to say that within the field of Catholic pastoral education there are only very few men who can claim for themselves the title of pastoral supervisor. To show the importance of supervision we will look at three of its characteristics.

1. An antiprojective regime

First of all supervision is an antiprojective regime. The most striking characteristic of supervision is the constant invitation to take back our projections. The centre of attention is the trainee. And although the trainee might explain his problems easily as the problem of the older pastor, the rigid institution, the unfatherly bishop, the anticlericalism of the students, the supervisor will ask him: 'But what about you?' There are many ways to project. But seldom are we made aware of our inclination to draw people or situations into the picture behind which we can hide ourselves. What the supervisor does is to bring us right back to the centre of the problem: me.

2. A school for alternatives

Secondly, supervision is a school for alternatives. Every pastor has his own strengths and qualities. It is obvious that he will use and develop them as best he can. One will feel at ease in the pulpit, another in the classroom, a third in youth groups and a fourth in individual counselling. The question is whether our qualities might not become temptations to narrow us down to only those fields to which we feel most inclined. Professional training means a training which broadens our ways of pastoring and offers us possible alternatives. It gives us the freedom to act differently in different situations based not just on our inclination but on the understanding of the particular situation. Through supervision we are invited to face the weaker aspects of our behaviour. The supervisor is saying: 'There are many ways of being a good pastor. I know that this is the way in which you feel most comfortable, which is most easy to you, so let us forget this way for a moment and have a look at other possible ways.' If a man uses his strong capacities too much he is in danger of having his other potentials become paralysed or at least underdeveloped. If he feels too much at ease with a specific pattern of behaviour the danger exists that the learning process will stop.

Supervision never gives lasting satisfaction. It is an ongoing process of opening new possibilities. This opening is a most painful process. It gives you the feeling that everything can be done differently and that it is at least immature not to consider the other possibilities.

Therefore, supervision seems to be only consistent in its inconsistencies. It forces one constantly to move away from what is safe. It is a very frustrating process. The supervisor often seems to consider his student as cream. He doesn't mind in what direction he churns him, he's only interested in the butter which is the result of all his stirring.

As a school for alternatives, supervision creates distance. It says: 'Stop, have a look at yourself, and think.' The tendency to act on the spur and the impulse of the moment is so great that blindness to alternatives can result. But after good supervision we know at least that although we are taking one road there are other roads which we did not choose. We know that distance is possible without causing separation, and that involvement is possible without causing blindness.

3. The way to basic questions

Finally, supervision is the way to ask the basic questions. Supervision is not a problem-solving device in which the supervisor advises his student what to do in difficult cases. It rather offers the freedom and opportunity to ask the basic questions. Very often the minister invests much time and energy in problems which are peripheral and accidental, without questioning the suppositions on which his actions are based. Many problems can be used to hide the real question. The question: What should I say to this student? can cover up the question: Why do I want to say something to him at all? The question: How can I reach as many students as possible? can cover up the question: Why should I reach so many students? The question: How can I make the liturgy attractive? can hide the question: What does attractiveness mean when speaking about liturgy? The question: How can I be a good witness for Christ? can disregard the question: Does Christ really mean anything to me? And finally the question: How can I be a good priest? can avoid the question: Do I really want to be a priest? Through supervision we might finally have the courage to touch the heart of the matter and to ask the basic questions. And this brings us back to where we started: Asking basic questions is the privilege of the mature Christian. So we see supervision as an antiprojective regime, as a school for alternatives and way to ask the basic questions.

[b] The pastoral experience

But what has to be supervised? That is our final problem. The answer seems simple: pastoral experience. But how does pastoral experience become available for supervision? By control, by creative limitation. Franz Alexander calls psychotherapy a controlled life experience. Training for the ministry can very well be called a controlled pastoral experience. Doing many different things can be helpful as well as damaging, but doing just a few things under close supervision is priceless. Talking with hundreds of people about God may be fine, but analysing one conversation word for word is a learning experience. Not only learning how to talk, but also learning how to understand myself in the interaction with my fellow man. The great importance of pastoral training is the opportunity for the minister to experience himself as a professional person in a controlled setting. To struggle with one's own professional self in a situation in which every aspect of one's daily ministerial practice becomes subject to supervision is a way of learning, unique and practically unknown in the tradition of Catholic theological education. It is especially the controlled experience which makes this pastoral experience different from so many other experiences in the field.

About a decade ago some Hollanders started to build a miniature Dutch city in which the tallest church tower did not come higher than a man's waist, the famous public buildings of the country were knee-high, the great rivers could be crossed in one step and the whole world in which we live could be overlooked in one glance. This miniature city soon became one of the greatest tourist attractions and not just for children as was planned, but for adults as well. The sensation seems to be the controlled life experience. People suddenly were able to see themselves as a part in a larger setting of which the structure and the boundaries were visible. This is what makes supervised pastoral experience so exciting. It is a pastoral experience in miniature, through which we are able to see where we stand and where we go. If we want to prepare ourselves to live and work in the complex university community it is important to start by looking at it from some distance and to make us familiar with the complex map of student life, so that we will not get lost, once we enter it fully.

We will finish as we started. The minister preparing himself for work on the campus is like an army chaplain entering the battlefield for the first time. Anticipatory anxiety is to be expected.

This anxiety can paralyse efficient work and endanger the integration of the personality but by careful training this same anxiety can become constructive instead of destructive and a source of great pastoral creativity instead of distress. A minister who is prepared for his task can enter a university community even when it is in great turmoil, without fear. He is free. With a realistic confidence in his abilities, with a sense of inner harmony and most of all with the trust in the value of his service, he can be a free witness for God, who can strengthen hope, fulfil love, and make joy complete.

Conclusion

Intimacy was the main theme which brought together the otherwise so different subjects of this book. In the context of man's development from the magic oneness of the small child to the faithful oneness of the adult Christian we discussed the intimate relationships possible between man and woman, man and man, man and God. We also tried to show the problem of the student trying to find his own place within the religious community and finally we analyzed the situation of the contemporary minister who is called to guide others in their search for meaning without losing his own home.

It does not seem an exaggeration to say that this book was primarily concerned about the inner life of man. This might seem a somewhat unpopular emphasis in a time in which the social problems are so pressing that much attention for the 'stirrings of the soul' easily suggests a pietistic preoccupation with the self.

But if man really has to love his neighbour as himself there seems to be a good reason to wonder if man today is able enough to relate to himself in a creative way and to live from the centre of his existence.

During the past years many concerned idealistic men returned from their social actions in the fields, the ghettos and the slums with the painful realization that the courage to continue and the will to persevere cannot depend on the gratification which they received from their involvement. There were hardly any visible results, very few words of thanks and not seldom suspicion and hostility. Many were thrown back on themselves and had to ask: 'Why should I do all this, when nobody asks me to do it, when many call me naive, and when most people remain completely indifferent towards my great desire to make a better world?' The answer to this question will never come unless man is able to live from his centre and feel at home with his own self. Consciously or unconsciously many young people practicing Yoga, reading Zen and intrigued by new forms of meditation are asking for a new spirituality and are looking for a guide.

The churches, in many ways entangled in their own structural problems, often seem hardly ready to respond to this growing need to live a spiritual life. The tragedy is that many find the church more in the way to God than the way to God, and are looking for religious experiences far away from the ecclesiastical institutions. But if we read the signs well, we are on the threshold of a new area of spiritual life, the nature and ramifications of which we can hardly foresee. Hopefully, we will not be distracted by the trivia of churchy family-quarrels and overlook the great questions which really matter. Hopefully, we will be sensitive enough to feel the gentle breeze by which God makes His presence known. (1 Kings 19:13).

A LETTER OF
CONSOLATION

Introduction

This letter was written six months after the death of my mother. I wrote it to my father as a letter of consolation. When I wrote it I did not think of making it public, but now, three years later, I feel a certain urge to do so. Because now I have a real desire to offer this letter to all those who suffer the pain that death can bring and who search for new life. During the last few years I have come to realize in a new way what it means to live and die for each other. As this awareness grew in me, I began to wonder if the fruits of our grief are to be tasted only by ourselves.

Like other letters, this letter has its own history and I would like to introduce its publication by offering some explanation of why I decided to write it.

Very shortly after my mother's funeral in October 1978, I returned from Holland to the United States. A few days later I was busy again, as always, teaching, counselling students, attending faculty meetings, answering mail and doing the many things that fill the daily life of a university teacher. There had been little or no opportunity to let mother's suffering and death enter deeply into my innermost self.

During the days that my mother was dying and during the days immediately after her death, I tried to pay as much attention as I could to my family and to anyone who offered friendship and love. And then, back in the United States, far away from home, the busy school life certainly did not encourage me to listen to my own inner cries. But one day, when I paused for a while in my office between appointments, I suddenly realized that I had not shed a single tear before or after mother's death. At that moment I saw that the world had such a grasp on me that it did not allow me to fully experience even the most personal, the most intimate, and the most mysterious event of my life. It seemed as if the voices around me were saying, 'You have to keep going. Life goes on; people die, but you must continue to live, to work, to struggle. The past cannot be recreated. Look at what is ahead.' I was obedient to these voices: I gave my lectures with the same enthusiasm as ever; I listened to students and their problems as if nothing had happened; and I worked with the same compulsiveness that had characterized my life since I started to teach. But I knew then that this would not last if I really took my mother and myself seriously. By a happy coincidence – no, by a gracious gift of God – I had planned a six months' retreat with the Trappist monks at the Abbey of the Genesee, which during the past years had become a second home to me.

When I arrived at the monastery in January I knew that this was going to be my time of grief. On several occasions, while sitting in my little room surrounded by the deep silence of the monastery, I noticed tears coming from my eyes. I did not really understand this. I was not thinking about mother, I was not remembering her illness, her death, or her funeral, but from a place in me deeper than I could reach, grief welled up and manifested itself in soft weeping.

As the days and weeks passed I experienced a growing urge to live through more fully and more directly the loss of which my tears reminded me. But I did not want to do this alone. I wanted to do it with someone who could really understand what was happening inside me. And who could better understand me than my own father? It was an obvious and easy decision, because ever since my mother's death his letters had become my greatest source of comfort. In these letters he had told me about his own grief and his struggle to build a new, meaningful life without her. Maybe I could offer him consolation and comfort by uniting my pain with his.

Thus, I started to write this letter to my father, a letter to speak with him about her whom we had both loved so much, a letter to show him my love and affection, a letter to offer him some of my reflections on mother's death – in short, a letter of consolation. I wrote and wrote and wrote. Once I started to write I realized how much I felt, how much I wanted to say, and how much had remained hidden during the six months since mother had died.

To whom did I write this letter? To my father, surely. But I was also writing to myself. Who was consoled? My father was, I know, but when I finally wrote down the last words, I knew that I had received as much and maybe more comfort and consolation than he would. Many letters are that way: they touch the writer as much as the receiver.

I now realize that this letter had to be written for my father, for me, and maybe, too, for many others who are asking the same questions that we were asking. When I asked my father, two and a half years after the letter was written, how he would feel about making it available to others in the form of a small book, he said, 'If you think that your writing about mother's death and about our grief can be a source of hope and consolation to more people than just ourselves, do not be afraid to have it printed.'

And thus, after some thought and much encouragement from friends, I felt that it would be good to take the letter out of the privacy of my life and that of my father and offer it to those who know the same darkness and are searching for the same light.

I hope and pray that I made the right decision.

Henri J. M. Nouwen
December 29, 1981

Dear Father

Next Monday it will be half a year since mother died. It will be Holy Week and both of us will be preparing ourselves to celebrate Easter. How will this Easter be for us? You will be in the parish church of our little Dutch town listening to the story of Christ's resurrection. I will read that same story to monks and guests in a Trappist monastery in upstate New York. Both of us will look at the Easter candle, symbol of the risen Christ, and think not only of him but also of her. Our minds and hearts will be flooded with ideas and feelings that are too deep, too complex, and too intimate to express. But I am sure that we both shall think about last year's Easter, when she was still with us. We both shall remember how she loved this great feast and how she decorated the house with flowers and the dinner table with purple and yellow ribbons. Somehow it seems long, long ago. Isn't that your experience also? The last six months could as well have been six years. Her death changed our experience of time; the short period between last October and this April seemed a very strange time in which the days, weeks and months were as long as they are for a small child who is taking his first steps. We had to relearn life. Every 'normal' experience became for us like a new experience. It had the quality of a 'first time'. How often have we used these words! The first Christmas without mother, the first New Year without mother, the first wedding anniversary without mother. And now it will be the first Easter without mother. I know that you have been asking yourself often, as I have, 'How will it be without her?' We can hardly remember any of these events without her being part of them. We can no longer predict how we will feel on these familiar days and occasions. They are, in fact, no longer familiar. They have become unknown to us. We have become suddenly aware how intimately our ideas, feelings, and perceptions were determined by her presence. Easter was not only an important day to celebrate, but a day to celebrate with her, a day on which her voice was heard, her letters anticipated, her active presence felt – so much so that we could not distinguish between the joys brought to us by the feast and the joys brought to us by her presence at the feast. They had become one and the same. But now we are forced to make a distinction, and now we have become like children who have to learn to do things for the first time on their own.

New experiences such as these have made the last six months a strange time for us. Her death became an ongoing death for us. Every time we lived through another event without her, we felt her absence in a new way. We became aware of deep connections with her that we had forgotten for a while but that were brought back to consciousness by the forward movement of history. And each time, she died again in us. Memories of what she would have done, said, or written on certain occasions made us more aware of her not being with us and deepened our grief.

Real grief is not healed by time. It is false to think that the passing of time will slowly make us forget her and take away our pain. I really want to console you in this letter, but not by suggesting that time will take away your pain, and that in one, two, three, or more years you will not miss her so much any more. I would not only be telling a lie, I would be diminishing the importance of mother's life, underestimating the depth of your grief, and mistakenly relativizing the power of the love that has bound mother and you together for forty-seven years. If time does anything, it deepens our grief. The longer we live, the more fully we become aware of who she was for us, and the more intimately we experience what her love meant for us. Real, deep love is, as you know, very unobtrusive, seemingly easy and obvious, and so present that we take it for granted. Therefore, it is often only in retrospect – or better, in memory – that we fully realize its power and depth. Yes, indeed, love often makes itself visible in pain. The pain we are now experiencing shows us how deep, full, intimate and all-pervasive her love was.

Is this a consolation? Does this bring comfort? It appears that I am doing the opposite of bringing consolation. Maybe so. Maybe these words will only increase your tears and deepen your grief. But for me, your son, who grieves with you, there is no other way. I want to comfort and console you, but not in a way that covers up real pain and avoids all wounds. I am writing you this letter in the firm conviction that reality can be faced and entered with an open mind and an open heart, and in the sincere belief that consolation and comfort are to be found where our wounds hurt most.

When I write to you, therefore, that, in our remembering, not only the full depth of mother's love but also the full pain of her leaving us will become known to us, I do so with the trying question in mind: 'Why is it that she died before we did and why is it that we are the ones who have to carry the burden of grief?' You must have asked yourself this question many times. You have lived your life with the unquestioned assumption that you would die before mother. You felt this way not simply because you were three years older than she or because her health always seemed better than yours, but because you sensed that she would be more capable of living on without you than you without her. Why then are you the one who has to relearn life without her, and why are you the one who came to know her not only in the joy of her presence but in the pain of her absence? She has been spared the sorrow of your death; she never had to experience life without you. All the sorrow has been given to you to bear, and you have been entrusted with that awesome task of discovering her love not only in life but in death. Why? Although I am twenty-nine years younger than you are, and although the 'logic of life' says parents die before their children, for me the question is no different, because love does not know 'clock time'.

I am writing this letter to you conscious of this great question. I want to explore with you and for you the meaning of her death and our life, of her life and our death. In your letters to me since her death – letters richer and fuller than any you wrote to me before – you have raised the question of death yourself. Ever since we saw her still face in the hospital, we have wondered what death really is. It is a question mother has left us with, and we want to face it, enter it, explore it, and let it grow in us. By doing so we may be able to console one another. It will be a hard road to travel, but if we travel it together we may have less to fear. I am glad, therefore, that in this quiet and peaceful Trappist monastery I have the opportunity to write you this letter, and I am especially glad that I can write to you during the days when both of us are preparing ourselves to celebrate the resurrection of our Lord Jesus Christ.

I

Often I feel sad about the great distance between us. Although I have always been content with living in the United States, since mother's death I have sensed more than before the distance that prevents me from being of more help and support to you during these difficult months. Regular letters and occasional phone calls are a very limited substitute for being together. And yet the paradox of it all is that the distance between us may prove after all to be a blessing in disguise. If I were still living in Holland and were able to visit you every weekend and call you every day, I should probably never have been able to let you know my deeper feelings about mother and you. Isn't it true that it is much harder to say deep things to each other than to write them? Isn't it much more frightening to express our deeper feelings about each other when we sit around the breakfast table than when the Atlantic Ocean separates us? We have spent many hours watching television together since mother died. We have often had a meal together at home or in a restaurant. We have taken little rides together through the woods. But seldom, very seldom, have we spoken about what was closest to our hearts. It was as if the physical closeness prevented the spiritual closeness we both desired. I am not sure if I fully understand this myself, but it seems that we are not the only people for whom this holds true. Physical and spiritual closeness are two quite different things, and they can – although they do not always – inhibit each other. The great distance between us may be enabling us to develop a relationship that you might not be able to develop with your other children and their families who live so close to you.

One obvious result of our distance is that you have started to write letters to me. Since mother died you not only write more often, but your letters are different. That has meant a lot to me during the last six months. I had become so used to mother's weekly letters, in which she told about all the family events, big and small, and kept showing her interest in my own life with all its ups and downs, that I feared their sudden absence. You used to write very seldom, and when you did, your letters consisted mostly of general, almost philosophical, reflections; they did not reveal much about your actual work, concerns, or feelings.

192

It always seemed as though you felt that mother was the one who took care of personal relationships. I remember how often you used to say, as I left the house to return to the United States, 'Don't forget to write to mother.' It was almost as if you were not very interested in hearing from me and were primarily concerned that mother and I would stay in close touch. I do not think that this was true. On the contrary, I think that you were very interested in hearing from me, but you usually left it to mother to express the affection, concern, and interest that you shared with her. Sometimes it was even humorous. Whenever I called you by phone, I was surprised that you took it for granted that I really called for mother. I always had the hardest time keeping you on the line for more than a few seconds. After reassuring me that everything was fine with you, you always said quickly, 'Well, here's mother.' I knew a call made you happy, but your happiness seemed to be derived from mother's joy and gratefulness.

But now she is no longer there for you to hide behind. And you have indeed stepped forward! You have written me letters as warm and personal as those of mother's. In fact, even more so. And just as I once looked forward to receiving mother's letters, I now long for yours. Now I not only know – as I did before – that you are interested in my life, but I can also see it expressed in your written words. And now you accept the simple and true fact that I write to you for yourself alone and call you for yourself alone.

The more I think about this, the more I realize that mother's death caused you to step forward in a way you could not before. Maybe there is even more to say than that. Maybe I have to say that you have found in yourself the capacity to be not only a father, but a mother as well. You have found in yourself that same gift of compassion that brought mother so much love and so much suffering. You have started to see more clearly the loneliness of your friends and to sympathize more with their search for company; you have begun to feel more deeply the fears of your widowed colleagues and to experience more sharply the mystery of death. And – if I may say so – you have discovered that you have a son who has been alone since he left your house. Becoming a priest for me has in fact meant to enter the road of 'the long loneliness', as Dorothy Day called it, and my many physical and spiritual journeys have deepened that experience even further. That long loneliness is what had made me feel so especially close to mother and has made me feel so lost by her death. But isn't this now also the basis for a unique solidarity between the two of us? Am I right when I suppose that you, who are known and feared for your irony and sarcasm, for your sharp wit and critical analysis – all qualities that made you such a good lawyer – are now allowing your tender side to come more to the centre and are now experiencing a new bond with those who are dear to you?

There is always that strange tendency in marriage to divide roles, even psychological roles. And our culture certainly encourages that: mother for the children, you for earning a living; mother to be gentle and forgiving, you to be strict and demanding; mother hospitable and receptive, you reserved and selective. In fact, you even liked to play with these differences and point them out in your comments at dinner. But now there are no longer any qualities to divide, and you are challenged to let develop more fully in yourself what you so admired in mother. I even sense that the memory of mother, and the way she lived her life with you, makes you consciously desire to let her qualities remain visible for your children and your friends – visible in you.

You are not imitating mother. You are not saying, 'I will do things the way mother used to do them.' That would be artificial and certainly not an honour to her. No, you are becoming more yourself, you are exploring those areas of life that always were part of you but remained somewhat dormant in mother's presence. I think that we both have a new and honourable task. It is the task to be father, son, and friend in a new way, a way that mother made possible not only through her life, but through her death. When Jesus said that if a grain of wheat dies it will yield a rich harvest, he not only spoke about his own death but indicated the new meaning he would give to our death. So we have to ask ourselves, 'Where do we see the harvest of mother's death?' There is no doubt in my mind that this harvest is becoming visible first of all in those who loved her most. Our deep love for her allows us to be the first to reap the harvest and to share with others the gifts of her death.

Isn't it here that we have to start if we want to discover the meaning of mother's death? Before anything else, we have to come into touch with – yes, even claim – the mysterious reality of new life in ourselves. Others might see it, feel it, and enjoy it before we do. That is why I am writing to you about it. We may help each other to see this new life. That would be true consolation. It would make us experience in the centre of our beings that the pain mother's death caused us has led us to a new way of being, in which the distance between mother, father, or child slowly dissolves. Thus our separation from mother brings us to a new inner unity and invites us to make that new unity a source of joy and hope for each other and for others as well.

2

As I said earlier, mother's death has made us raise more directly and explicitly the question of death itself. The question about death, however, is mostly asked by someone who is himself not dying. You yourself made me aware of this when you reminded me how much mother spoke about her death when there was no real danger and yet hardly mentioned it at all when she was actually dying. It seems indeed important that we face death before we are in any real danger of dying and reflect on our mortality before all our conscious and unconscious energy is directed to the struggle to survive. It is important to be prepared for death, very important; but if we start thinking about it only when we are terminally ill, our reflections will not give us the support we need. We enjoy good health now. We are asking about death, mother's death and our own, not because we are dying, but because we feel strong enough to raise the question about our most basic human infirmity.

I want to take up the challenge of this question. This indeed seems to be the opportune time not only for you, but also for me. We both have to ask ourselves what mother's death means, and we both are confronted in a new way with our own deaths. The fact that you are 'already' seventy-six and I am 'only' forty-seven is not a real hindrance to a common meditation on death. I think, in fact, that mother's death has taken away much of the age difference between us, so that the prospect of dying and death is not really different for you and for me. Once you have reached the top of the mountain, it does not make much difference at which point on the way down you take a picture of the valley – as long as you are not in the valley itself.

I think, then, that our first task is to befriend death. I like that expression 'to befriend'. I first heard it used by Jungian analyst James Hillman when he attended a seminar I taught on Christian Spirituality at Yale Divinity School. He emphasized the importance of 'befriending': befriending your dreams, befriending your shadow, befriending your unconscious. He made it convincingly clear that in order to become full human beings, we have to claim the totality of our experience; we come to maturity by integrating not only the light but also the dark side of our story into our selfhood. That made a lot of sense to me, since I am quite familiar with my own inclination, and that of others, to avoid, deny, or suppress the painful side of life, a tendency that always leads to physical, mental or spiritual disaster.

And isn't death, the frightening unknown that lurks in the depths of our unconscious minds, like a great shadow that we perceive only dimly in our dreams? Befriending death seems to be the basis of all other forms of befriending. I have a deep sense, hard to articulate, that if we could really befriend death we would be free people. So many of our doubts and hesitations, ambivalences and insecurities are bound up with our deep-seated fear of death that our lives would be significantly different if we could relate to death as a familiar guest instead of a threatening stranger.

In the book *Nacht und Nebel*, the Dutchman Floris Bakels writes about his experiences in the German prisons and concentration camps of the Second World War. He makes very clear what power a man can have who has befriended his own death. I know how much this book has moved you, and I was very happy with the copy I just received. Wouldn't you say that Floris Bakels was able to survive the horrors of Dachau and other camps and write about it thirty-two years later precisely because he had befriended death? It seems, at least to me, that Floris Bakels said in many different ways to his SS captors, 'You have no power over me, because I have already died.' Fear of death often drives us into death, but by befriending death, we can face our mortality and choose life freely.

But how do we befriend death? During the last few years you have seen many deaths – even of people you knew quite well. They have touched you, shocked you, surprised you, and even caused you grief, but when mother died it seemed as if death came to you for the first time. Why? I think because love – deep, human love – does not know death. The way you and mother had become one, and the way this oneness had deepened itself during forty-seven years of marriage, did not allow termination. Real love says, 'Forever'. Love will always reach out towards the eternal. Love comes from that place within us where death cannot enter. Love does not accept the limits of hours, days, weeks, months, years, or centuries. Love is not willing to be imprisoned by time.

That is why mother's death was such a totally different experience for you from the deaths of so many other people you have known. In the core of your being, you – your love – could not accept her leaving you so drastically, so radically, so totally, and so irretrievably. Her death went directly against your most profound intuitions. And so I could well understand your writing to me that mother's death had led you to the general question of death's meaning. Someone might say, 'Why did it take him so long to raise that question? He is seventy-six years old – and only now does he wonder about the meaning of death.' But someone who says this does not understand that only mother could raise that question for you, because in her dying the real absurdity of death revealed itself to you. Only her death could really make you protest in your innermost being and make you cry out, 'Why could our love not prevent her from dying?'

Yet, the same love that reveals the absurdity of death also allows us to befriend death. The same love that forms the basis of our grief is also the basis of our hope; the same love that makes us cry out in pain also must enable us to develop a liberating intimacy with our own most basic brokenness. Without faith, this must sound like a contradiction. But our faith in Him whose love overcame death and who rose from the grave on the third day converts this contradiction into a paradox, the most healing paradox of our existence. Floris Bakels experienced this in a unique way. He came to see and feel that the power of love is stronger than the power of death and that it is indeed true that 'God is love'. Surrounded by people dying from hunger, torture and total exhaustion, and knowing quite well that any hour could be his hour to die, he found in the core of his being a love so strong and so profound that the fear of death lost its power over him. For Floris Bakels, this love was not a general feeling or emotion, nor an idea about a benevolent Supreme Being. No, it was the very concrete, real, and intimate love of Jesus Christ, Son of God and redeemer of the world. With his whole being he knew that he was loved with an infinite love, held in an eternal embrace and surrounded by an unconditional care. This love was so concrete, so tangible, so direct, and so close for him that the temptation to interpret this religious experience as the fantasy of a starved mind had no lasting hold on him. The more deeply and fully he experienced Christ's love, the more he came to see that the many loves in his life – the love of his parents, his brothers and sisters, his wife, and his friends – were reflections of the great 'first' love of God.

I am convinced that it was the deeply felt love of God – felt in and through Jesus Christ – that allowed Floris Bakels to face his own death and the deaths of others so directly. It was this love that gave him the freedom and energy to help people in agony and made it possible for him to resume a normal life after he returned from the hell of Dachau.

I am writing so much about Bakels because I know that you, being of the same generation and the same profession, can understand him quite well and will lend him a sympathetic ear. He can indeed show you better than psychologists or psychoanalysts what it means to befriend death.

Although you and I also tasted the terror of the Nazis, you as a young man who had to hide yourself to escape from deportation and I as a fearful child, and although we all had to struggle hard to keep alive during the horrible 'winter of hunger' in

1944–45, we were spared the horrors of the concentration camps and did not have to face death in the way Floris Bakels did. Thus, we were not forced to befriend death at such an early age. But mother's death invites us to do so now. Many people seem never to befriend death and die as if they were losing a hopeless battle. But we do not have to share that sad fate. Mother's death can bring us that freedom of which Bakels writes; it can make us deeply aware that her love was a reflection of a love that does not and cannot die – the love that we both will affirm again on Easter Sunday.

3

In no way do I want to suggest that you have been repressing or denying your mortality. In fact, I know few people who have been so open about their own death. At different times you have spoken about your own death publicly and privately, to strangers and to friends, mockingly and seriously. Sometimes you even embarrassed mother and your guests with your directness! I remember your mentioning on several occasions how quickly our 'great lives' are forgotten and how short-lived are the pious memories of our friends and colleagues. I remember how you told me, before you left on a long trip to Brazil, what I should do in case a fatal accident took the lives of you both. And I remember your very concrete wishes about the way you hoped your children and friends would respond to your death. Sometimes your words about your death had a sarcastic quality, and conveyed a desire to unmask sentimentalism and false romanticism. You even enjoyed gently shocking the pious feelings of your friends and testing your and their sense of reality. But mostly, your words were serious and showed that you were indeed reflecting on the end of your own life. Thus it is quite clear that you have not been living as if your life would go on forever. You are too intelligent and too realistic for that.

Still, hidden in us there are levels of not-knowing, not-understanding and not-feeling that can only be revealed to us in our moments of great crisis. For some people such moments never come, for others they come frequently. For some they come early, for others they come quite late. We might think that we have a certain insight into 'what life is all about' until an unexpected crisis throws us off balance and forces us to rethink our most basic presuppositions. In fact, we never really know how deeply our lives are anchored, and the experience of crisis can open up dimensions of life that we never knew existed.

Mother's death is certainly one of the most crucial experiences of both our lives, perhaps even the most crucial. Before her death, it was impossible to know even vaguely what it would do to us. Now we are beginning to sense its impact. Gradually we are able to see where it is leading us. A new confrontation with death is taking place, a confrontation that we could never have created ourselves. Whatever we felt, said, or thought about death in the past was always within the reach of our own emotional or intellectual capacities. In a certain sense, it remained within the range of our own influence and control. Remarks and ideas about our own deaths remained *our* remarks and *our* ideas and were therefore subject to our own inventiveness and originality. But mother's death was totally outside the field of our control or influence. It left us powerless. When we saw how slowly she lost contact with us and fell away from us, we could do nothing but stand beside her bed and watch death exercise its ruthless power. This experience is not an experience for which we can really prepare ourselves. It is so new and so overpowering that all of our previous speculations and reflections seem trivial and superficial in the presence of the awesome reality of death. Thus mother's death changes the question of death into a new question. It opens us to levels of life that could not have been reached before, even if we had had the desire to reach them.

What did mother's death do to you? I do not know and cannot know since it is something so intimate that nobody can enter fully into your emotions. But if your experience of her death is in any way close to mine, you were 'invited' – as I was – to re-evaluate your whole life. Mother's death made you stop and look back in a way you had not done before. Suddenly you entered into a situation that made you see your many years of life – your life as a student, a young professional, a successful lawyer, a well-known professor – with a bird's-eye view. I remember your telling me how you could capture your long and complex history in one clear picture, and how from the point of view of mother's death, your life lost much of its complexity and summarized itself in a few basic lines. In that way her death gave you new eyes with which to see your own life and helped you to distinguish between the many accidental aspects and the few essential elements.

Death indeed simplifies; death does not tolerate endless shadings and nuances. Death lays bare what really matters, and in this way becomes your judge. It seems that we both have experienced this after mother's death and funeral. During the last six months we have been reviewing our life with mother. For you this meant opening drawers that had not been opened for years; looking at photographs whose very existence you had forgotten; reading old letters now yellow and wrinkled with age; and picking up books that had collected much dust on the shelves. For me this meant re-reading her letters to me; looking again at the gifts she brought to me on visits; and praying with renewed attention the psalms we so often prayed together. Long-forgotten events returned to memory as if they had taken place only recently. It seemed as if we could put our whole lives in the palms of our hands like small precious stones and gaze at them with tenderness and admiration. How tiny, how beautiful, how valuable!

I think that from the point of view of mother's death and our own mortality, we can now see our lives as a long process of mortification. You are familiar with that word. Priests use it a lot during Lent. They say, 'You have to mortify yourself.' It sounds unpleasant and harsh and moralistic. But mortification – literally, 'making death' – is what life is all about, a slow discovery of the mortality of all that is created so that we can appreciate its beauty without clinging to it as if it were a lasting possession. Our lives can indeed be seen as a process of becoming familiar with death, as a school in the art of dying. I do not mean this in a morbid way. On the contrary, when we see life constantly relativized by death, we can enjoy it for what it is: a free gift. The pictures, letters, and books of the past reveal life to us as a constant saying of farewell to beautiful places, good people, and wonderful experiences. Look at the pictures of your children when you could play with them on the floor of the living room. How quickly you had to say goodbye to them! Look at the snapshots of your bike trips with mother in Brittany in the mid-thirties. How few were the summers in which those trips were possible! Read mother's letters when you were in Amalfi recuperating from your illness and my letters to you from my first trip to England. They speak now of fleeting moments. Look at the wedding pictures of your children and at the Bible I gave you on the day of my ordination. All these times have passed by like friendly visitors, leaving you with dear memories but also with the sad recognition of the shortness of life. In every arrival there is a leave-taking; in every reunion there is a separation; in each one's growing up there is a growing old; in every smile there is a tear; and in every success there is a loss. All living is dying and all celebration is mortification too.

Although this was happening all the time during our rich and varied lives, we did not notice it with the same acuteness as we do now. There was so much life, so much vitality, and so much exuberance that the presence of death was less striking and was only acknowledged in the way we acknowledge our shadows on a sunny day. There were moments of pain, sadness, disillusionment; there were illnesses, setbacks, conflicts and worries. But they came and went like the seasons of the year, and the forces of life always proved victorious. Then mother died. Her death was a definitive end, a total break that presented itself with a finality unlike any other. For a while, we kept living as if she were only gone for a time and could return at any moment. We even kept doing things as if we were preparing for the moment when she would appear again on our doorsteps. But as the days passed, our hearts came to know that she was gone, never to return. And it was then that real grief began to invade us. It was then that we turned to the past and saw that death had been present in our lives all along and that the many farewells and goodbyes had been pointing to this dark hour. And it was then that we raised in a wholly new way the question of the meaning of death.

4

When we experienced the deep loss at mother's death, we also experienced our total inability to do anything about it. We, who loved mother so much and would have done anything possible to alleviate her pain and agony, could do absolutely nothing. All of us who stood around her bed during her last days felt powerless. Sometimes we looked at the doctors and nurses with the vain hope that maybe *they* could change the course of events, but we realized that what we were witnessing was the inevitable reality of death, a reality we shall all have to face one day soon.

I think it is important for us to allow this experience of powerlessness in the face of mother's death to enter deeply into our souls, because it holds the key to a deeper understanding of the meaning of death.

Father, you are a man with a strong personality, a powerful will, and a convincing sense of self. You are known as a hard worker, a persistent fighter for your clients, and a man who never loses an argument, or at least will never confess to losing one! You have achieved what you strove for. Your successful career has rewarded your efforts richly and has strengthened you in your conviction that success in life is the result of hard work. If anything is clear about your life-style, it is that you want to keep your hands on the tiller of your ship. You like to be in control, able to make your own decisions and direct your own course. Experience has taught you that displaying weakness does not create respect and that it is safer to bear your burden in secret than to ask for pity. You never strove for power and influence, and even refused many positions that would have given you national recognition, but you fiercely guarded your own spiritual, mental and economic autonomy. Not only did you in fact achieve an impressive amount of autonomy for yourself, but you also encouraged your children to become free and independent people as soon as possible. I think it was this great value you put on autonomy that made you proud to see me leave for the United States. I am sure you did not want me to be so far from home, but this inconvenience was richly compensated for by the joy you drew from my ability to 'make it' independently of the support of my family and friends. One of your most often repeated remarks to me and to my brothers and sister was, 'Be sure not to become dependent on the power, influence, or money of others. Your freedom to make your own decisions is your greatest possession. Do not ever give that up.'

This attitude – an attitude greatly admired by mother and all of us in the family – explains why anything that reminded you of death threatened you. You found it very hard to be ill, you were usually a bit irritated with the illnesses of others, and you had very little sympathy for people whom you considered 'failures'. The weak did not attract you.

Mother's death opened up for you a dimension of life in which the key word is not autonomy, but surrender. In a very deep and existential way, her death was a frontal attack on your feeling of autonomy and independence, and in this sense, a challenge to conversion, that is, to the profound turning around of your priorities. I am not saying that mother's death made your autonomy and independence less valuable, but only that it put them into a new framework, the framework of life as a process of detachment.

Autonomy and detachment are not necessarily opposites. They can be if they confront each other on the same level of existence. But I sincerely believe that a healthy autonomy can give you the real strength to detach yourself when it is necessary to do so. Let me try to explain what I mean.

Even when we are trying to be in control and to determine our own course in life, we have to admit that life remains the great unknown to us. Although you worked quite hard in life to build up a successful career and to give your family a happy home, some of the main factors that made things develop the way they did were totally out of your hands. Many things that happened *to* you were as important as the things that happened *through* you. Fifty years ago, neither you nor anyone else could have predicted your present situation. And how futile it is for us to predict our own immediate or distant future. Things that made us worry greatly later prove to be quite insignificant, and things to which we hardly gave a thought before they took place turn our lives around. Thus our autonomy is rooted in unknown soil. This constitutes the great challenge: to be so free that we can be obedient, to be so autonomous that we can be dependent, to be so in control that we can surrender ourselves. Here we touch the great paradox in life: to live in order to be able to die. That is what detachment is all about. Detachment is not the opposite of autonomy but its fruit. It takes a good driver to know when to use his brakes!

This is far from theoretical, as you well know. We have both seen how some of our friends could not accept unforeseen changes in their lives and were unable to deal with an unknown future. When things went differently than they had expected or took a drastic turn, they did not know how to adjust to the new situation. Sometimes they became bitter and sour. Often they clung to familiar patterns of living that were no longer adequate and kept repeating what once made sense but no longer could speak to the real circumstances of the moment. Death has often affected people in this way, as we know too well. The death of husband, wife, child or friend can cause people to stop living towards the unknown future and make them withdraw into the familiar past. They keep holding on to a few precious memories and customs and see their lives as having come to a standstill. They start to live as if they were thinking, 'For me it is all over. There is nothing more to expect from life.' As you can see, here the opposite of detachment is taking place; here is a re-attachment that makes life stale and takes all vitality out of existence. It is a life in which hope no longer exists.

If mother's death were to lead us onto that road, her death would have no real meaning for us. Her death would be or become for us a death that closes the future and makes us live the rest of our lives in the enclosure of our own past. Then, our experience of powerlessness would not give us the freedom to detach ourselves from the past, but would imprison us in our own memories and immobilize us. Thus we would also lose the autonomy you have always held so dear.

I think there is a much more human option. It is the option to re-evaluate the past as a continuing challenge to surrender ourselves to an unknown future. It is the option to understand our experience of powerlessness as an experience of being guided, even when we do not know exactly where. Remember what Jesus said to Peter when he appeared to him after his resurrection: 'When you were young you put on your own belt and walked where you liked; but when you grow old you will stretch out your hands, and somebody else will put a belt round you and take you where you would rather not go.' Jesus said this immediately after he had told Peter three times to look after his sheep. Here we can see that a growing surrender to the unknown is a sign of spiritual maturity and does not take away autonomy. Mother's death is indeed an invitation to surrender ourselves more freely to the future, in the conviction that one of the most important parts of our lives may still be ahead of us and that mother's life and death were meant to make this possible. Do not forget that only after Jesus' death could his disciples fulfil their vocation.

I am constantly struck by the fact that those who are most detached from life, those who have learned through living that there is nothing and nobody in this life to cling to, are the really creative people. They are free to move constantly away from the familiar, safe places and can keep moving forward to new, unexplored areas of life. I am not suggesting to you that you are called to do something unusual or spectacular in your old age – although there is no telling to what you might be called! But I am thinking primarily of a spiritual process by which we can live our lives more freely than before, more open to God's guidance and more willing to respond when he speaks to our innermost selves.

Mother's death encourages us to give up the illusions of immortality we might still have and to experience in a new way our total dependence on God's love, a dependence that does not take away our free selfhood but purifies and ennobles it. Here you may catch a glimpse of the answer to the question of why mother died before you and why you have been given new years to live. Now you can say things to yourself, to others, and to God that were not disclosed to you before.

5

In all the previous reflections, dear father, an idea has emerged that was only vaguely in my mind when I started to write. It is the idea that the meaning of death is not so much the meaning our death has for us as the meaning it has for others. That explains why the meaning of mother's death and the meaning of our death are so closely related. I have a feeling that to the degree we can experience the fact that mother died for you, for her children, and for many others, our own death will have more meaning for us. I will try to explain this to you in such a way that you can find a certain obviousness in this idea.

Let me start with your own observation, which you have often made since mother's death, namely, that she lived her life for others. The more you reflected on her life, looked at her portraits, read her letters, and listened to what others said about her, the more you realized how her whole life was lived in the service of other people. I too am increasingly impressed by her attentiveness to the needs of others. This attitude was so much a part of her that it hardly seems remarkable. Only now can we see its full power and beauty. She rarely asked attention for herself. Her interest and attention went out to the needs and concerns of others. She was open to those who came to her. Many found it easy to talk with her about themselves and remarked how much at ease they had felt in her presence. This was especially noticeable during her visits to me in the United States. Often she knew my students better after one evening than I did after a year, and for many years to come she would keep asking about them. During the last six months I have grown painfully aware of how accustomed I had become to her unceasing interest in all that I did, felt, thought or wrote, and how much I had taken it for granted that, even if nobody else cared, she certainly did. The absence of that caring attention often gives me a deep feeling of loneliness. I know that this is even truer for you. You no longer hear her ask how well you slept, what your plans are for the day, or what you are writing about. You no longer hear her advise you to be careful on the road, to eat more, or to get some extra sleep. All these simple but so supportive and healing ways of caring are no longer there, and in their absence we begin to feel more and more what it means to be alone.

What I want to say now, however, is that she who lived for others also died for others. Her death should not be seen as a sudden end to all her care, as a great halt to her receptivity to others. There are people who experience the death of someone they love as a betrayal. They feel rejected, left alone, and even fooled. They seem to say to their husband, wife or friend, 'How could you do this to me? Why did you leave me behind in this way? I never bargained for this!' Sometimes people even feel angry towards those who die, and express this by a paralysing grief, by a regression to a state of total dependence, by all sorts of illnesses and complaints, and even by dying themselves.

If, however, mother's life was indeed a life lived for us, we must be willing to accept her death as a death for us, a death that is not meant to paralyse us, make us totally dependent, or provide an excuse for all sorts of complaints, but a death that should make us stronger, freer and more mature. To say it even more drastically: we must have the courage to believe that her death was good for us and that she died so that we might live. This is quite a radical viewpoint and it might offend the sensitivities of some people. Why? Because, in fact, I am saying, 'It is good for us that she left us, and to the extent that we do not accept this we have not yet fully understood the meaning of her life.' This might sound harsh and even offensive, but I believe deeply that it is true. Indeed, I believe even more deeply that we will come to experience this ourselves.

Although the time is past when widows were burned with their dead husbands – even a contemporary Phileas Fogg would not encounter such a scene on a trip around the world – still, in a psychological sense, many widows and widowers end their lives with that of their spouse. They respond to the death of husband or wife with a sudden lack of vitality and behaviour that turns life into a gruesome waiting room for death. I am aware of the fact that the other extreme – living on as if one had never been married – can also be seen. But since that is not within the horizon of our capacities, I do not need to talk about that here. What is important for us to recognize is that mother's own life invites us to see her death as a death that can bring us not only grief but also joy, not only pain but also healing, not only the experience of having lost but also the experience of having found.

This viewpoint is not just my personal viewpoint as against the viewpoint of others. It is the Christian viewpoint, that is, a viewpoint based on the life and death and resurrection of Jesus Christ. I need to be very clear about this, or you might not really understand what I am trying to express.

Five days have passed since I began this letter and it is now the evening before Holy Thursday. During this Holy Week we are confronted with death more than during any other season of the liturgical year. We are called to meditate not just on death in general or on our own death in particular, but on the death of Jesus Christ who is God and man. We are challenged to look at Him dying on a cross and to find there the meaning of our own life and death. What strikes me most in all that is read and said during these days is that Jesus of Nazareth did not die for Himself, but for us, and that in following Him we too are called to make our death a death for others. What makes you and me Christians is not only our belief that He who was without sin died for our sake on the cross and thus opened for us the way to His heavenly Father, but also that through His death our death is transformed from a totally absurd end of all that gives life its meaning into an event that liberates us and those whom we love. It is because of the liberating death of Christ that I dare say to you that mother's death is not simply an absurd end to a beautiful, altruistic life. Rather, her death is an event that allows her altruism to yield a rich harvest. Jesus died so that we might live, and everyone who dies in union with Him participates in the life-giving power of His death. Thus we can indeed say that mother, who died under the sign of the cross, died so that we might live. Therefore, under that same sign, each of our deaths can become a death for others. I think that we need to start seeing the profound meaning of this dying for each other in and through the death of Christ in order to catch a glimpse of what eternal life might mean. Eternity is born in time, and every time someone dies whom we have loved dearly, eternity can break into our mortal existence a little bit more.

I am aware that I am barely touching the great mystery I want to give words to. But I think that the mystery is so deep and vast that we can enter it only slowly and with great care.

As we enter more deeply into the mysteries of this Holy Week and come closer to Easter, it will become clear what needs to be said. But now it seems of first importance to realize that when we begin seeing that mother died for us, we can also catch an insight into the meaning of our own death. Initially this insight might well be that the meaning of our death cannot be expressed in an idea, a concept, or a theory. Rather, it must be discovered as a truth less visible to us than to those for whom we die. This is perhaps why the meaning of mother's death is slowly revealing itself to us even though it remained hidden from her, and why the meaning of our death will remain more concealed from us than from those who will miss us most. To die for others implies that the meaning of our death is better understood by them than by ourselves. This requires of us great detachment and even greater faith. But most of all, it calls us to an ever increasing surrender to the ways in which God chooses to manifest His love to us.

6

Today is Holy Thursday or, as you would say, White Thursday. As I continue this letter, I realize that this day enables me to write about death in a way that I could not before. As you know, Holy Thursday is the day of the Eucharist, the day on which Jesus took bread and wine and said to His intimate companions: 'Take ... eat ... drink ... this is my body ... this is my blood ... do this as a memorial of me.' On the night before His death, Jesus gave us the gift of His lasting presence in our midst in order to remind us in the most personal way that His death was a death for us. That is why Paul remarks in his letter to the Corinthians, 'Every time you eat this bread and drink this cup, you are proclaiming his death.'

I am glad that I can write to you about mother's death and about our own death on this holy day because now I can see more clearly than ever how much the mystery of this day binds us together. My whole being is rooted in the Eucharist. For me, to be a priest means to be ordained to present Christ every day as food and drink to my fellow Christians. I sometimes wonder if those who are close to me are sufficiently aware of the fact that the Eucharist constitutes the core of my life. I do so many other things and have so many secondary identities – teacher, speaker and writer – that it is easy to consider the Eucharist as the least important part of my life. But the opposite is true. The Eucharist is the centre of my life and everything else receives its meaning from that centre. I am saying this with so much emphasis in the hope that you will understand what I mean when I say that my life must be a continuing proclamation of the death and resurrection of Christ. It is first and foremost through the Eucharist that this proclamation takes place.

What has all of this to do with mother's death and with our death? A great deal, I think. Certainly much more than we might realize. You know better than I how important the Eucharist was for mother. There were few days in her adult life when she did not go to Mass and Communion. Although she did not speak much about it herself, we all knew that her daily participation in the Eucharist was at the centre of her life. There were few things that remained so constant in her daily routine. Wherever she was or whatever she did, she always tried to find a nearby church to receive the gifts of Christ. Her great desire for this daily spiritual nourishment frequently led you to plan your trips in such a way that you both could attend Mass each day before resuming your travels.

I do not think I am exaggerating when I say that it was mother's deep and lasting devotion to the Eucharist that was one of the factors, if not the main factor, in my decision to become a priest. That is why this Holy Thursday is such an important day. It unites us in a very intimate way. The death of Christ as proclaimed in the Eucharist has given meaning to our lives in a way too deep for us to explain. What is important is the realization that through participation in the Eucharist, our lives and our deaths are being lifted up in the life and death of Christ. This is an enormously mysterious reality, but the more deeply we enter into it the more comfort and consolation we will find during these months of grief. Long before you, mother, or I was born, the death of Christ was celebrated in the Eucharist. And it will be celebrated long after we have died. During our few years of conscious participation in the Eucharist, our lives and deaths become part of this ongoing proclamation of the life and death of Christ. Therefore I dare to say that every time I celebrate the Eucharist and every time you receive the body and blood of Christ, we remember not only Christ's death but also her death, because it was precisely through the Eucharist that she was so intimately united with Him.

This illuminates more fully that, in and through Christ, mother's death was a death for you and for me. By being united with Christ in the Eucharist, she participated in His life-giving death. Only Christ, the Son of God, could die not for Himself but for others. Mother's brokenness and sinfulness did not make it possible for her to die for others in complete self-surrender. But by eating the body and drinking the blood of Christ, her life was transformed into the life of Christ, and her death was lifted up into His death so that, living with Christ, she could also die with Him. Thus, it is the death of Christ that gives meaning to her death. Hence we can say quite boldly that she died for us. Perhaps the sentence, 'Christ died for us' has never before touched us in its full significance and has remained a rather abstract idea for both of us. But I think that mother's death can give us new insight into this central mystery of our faith. Once it starts making sense to us that mother died for our sake, and once we see that this was possible because of her intimate union with Christ through the Eucharist, we may also discover in a more personal way the ultimate meaning of Christ's death. Mother's death, then, directs our attention to the death of Christ and invites us to find in Him the source of all our consolation and comfort.

I do not think that you would have said any of the things I have tried to say today. The language I have used does not come easily to you and the words are probably not the words you yourself would use. But on the other hand, I know that what I have written is not unfamiliar to you. Although you shared in mother's devotion to the Eucharist during her lifetime and joined her regularly in receiving the body and blood of Christ, during the last six months you have come to realize that you can experience a lasting bond with her through this great sacrament. It is my great hope that you will find an increasing strength from the Eucharist. Since you are living alone and often experience painful loneliness, the gifts of Christ, who died for you, can unite you in a very intimate way with Him and so reveal to you the deeper meaning of mother's death. The Eucharist can never be fully explained or understood. It is a mystery to enter and experience from within. Every event of life can lead us to a deeper knowledge of the Eucharist. Marriage enables us to understand more deeply God's faithful love as it expresses itself in His lasting presence among us; illness and inner struggle can bring us more closely in touch with the healing power of the Eucharist; sin and personal failure can lead us to experience the Eucharist as a sacrament of forgiveness. What I am trying to say today is that mother's death can open our eyes to the Eucharist as a sacrament by which we proclaim Christ's death as a death for us, a death by which we are led to new life. Thus it can also help us to prepare for our own deaths. The more we see the Eucharist as a proclamation of Christ's death, the more we start seeing that our own deaths in communion with Christ cannot be in vain.

Thus the Eucharist brings us together in a very profound way. It is the core of my priesthood; it reveals the deeper meaning of mother's death; it helps us to prepare ourselves for our own deaths; and it points above all to Christ, who gives us His body and blood as a constant reminder that death is no longer a reason for despair but has become in and through Him the basis of our hope. Therefore we will have the boldness to sing tomorrow in the liturgy, 'We greet you cross, our only hope.'

7

It might be that after all my words about the meaning of death you will get the impression that death is something to be desired; something that we can journey towards with expectation; something for which all of life prepares us; something, therefore, that is more or less the high point of life. If I have created such an impression, I need to correct it as soon as I can. Although I think it is possible to speak about the meaning of death, I also think that death is the one event against which we protest with all our being. We feel that life belongs to us and that death has no place in our basic desire to live. It is therefore not so surprising that most people, even older people, do not think much about death. As long as we feel healthy and vital, we prefer to keep our minds and bodies busy with the things of life. German theologian Karl Rahner calls death 'the absurd arch-contradiction of existence' and indeed death does not make sense for anyone who can only make sense out of what he or she can understand in some way. But our total powerlessness in the face of death, in which any possibility of controlling our destiny is taken away from us, can hardly be perceived as having any value. Our whole being protests against the threat of non-being.

I am writing this on Good Friday. I have just participated in the liturgy, in which the death of Christ is remembered in the most moving way. I was asked to read the words Christ spoke during His passion. As I was pronouncing them in a loud voice so that all the monks and guests would be able to let them enter deeply into their hearts, I came to realize that Christ Himself entered with us into the full experience of the absurdity of death. Jesus did not want to die. Jesus did not face His death as if He considered it a good to be striven for. He never spoke about death as something to be accepted gladly. Although He spoke about His death and tried to prepare His disciples for it, He never gave it morbid attention. And the Gospels contain no evidence that death was attractive to Him. What we see in them is, rather, a deep inner protest against death. In the garden of Gethsemane, Jesus was gripped with fear and distress, and He prayed loudly to His Father: 'Everything is possible for you. Take this cup away from me.' This anguish became so intense that 'his sweat fell to the ground like great drops of blood'. And as He died on the Cross he cried out in agony: 'My God, my God, why have you deserted me?'

Much more than the pain of His death, I think, it was death itself that filled Jesus with fear and agony. For me this is a very important realization, because it undercuts any sentimentalizing or romanticizing of death. We do not want to die, even if we have to face – yes, befriend – our own death with all possible realism. Although we must befriend our death, that is, fully recognize it as a reality that is an intimate part of our humanity, death remains our enemy. Although we can and must prepare ourselves for death, we are never prepared for it. Although we have to see how death has been part of our life since birth, it remains the greatest unknown in our existence. Although we have to search for the meaning of death, our protest against it reveals that we will never be able to give it a meaning that can take our fear away.

Mother's death has made this very clear to us. You know how much her life was filled with the thought of God and His mysteries. Not only did she receive the Eucharist every day, but she spent many hours in prayer and meditation and read the holy Scriptures eagerly; she was also deeply grateful to everyone who supported her in her spiritual life. She had a very deep devotion to Mary, the Mother of God, and never went to sleep without asking for her prayers at the hour of her death. Indeed, mother's life was a life of preparation for death. But this did not make death easy for her. She never hesitated to say that she was afraid to die, that she did not feel prepared to appear before God, and that she was not yet ready to leave this world. She loved life, loved it to the full. She loved you with an unwavering devotion. You are the person she always thought of and spoke about first; she would never allow anyone to distract her attention from you. Her children and grandchildren were her perennial concern and delight. Their joys were her joys, and their pains were her pains. And how she loved beauty: the beauty of nature and its flowers and trees, mountains and valleys; the beauty of the French cathedrals or old village churches; the beauty of the Italian cities, Ravenna, Florence, Assisi and Rome. She could walk through these towns and cities and say with amazement, 'Look, isn't it beautiful, look at that house, look at that church, look at those balconies with bougainvillea – isn't it lovely!' And she would be filled with joy and amazement. Yes, mother loved life. I still remember how she said to me, 'Although I am old, I would like so much to live a few more years.'

Death was hard and painful for her. In fact, I often think that it was precisely because her life of prayer had given her such a profound appreciation of all that is created, that it was so very hard for her to let it all go. The God she loved and for whom she wanted to give her life had shown her both the splendour of His creation and the complete finality with which death would cut her off from all she had learned to love.

As I reflect on mother's death, something that I could not see as clearly before is now becoming more visible to me. It is that death does not belong to God. God did not create death. God does not want death. God does not desire death for us. In God there is no death. God is a God of life. He is the God of the living and not of the dead. Therefore, people who live a deeply spiritual life, a life of real intimacy with God, must feel the pain of death in a particularly acute way. A life with God opens us to all that is alive. It makes us celebrate life; it enables us to see the beauty of all that is created; it makes us desire to always be where life is. Death, therefore, must be experienced by a really religious person neither as a release from the tension of life nor as an occasion for rest and peace, but as an absurd, ungodly, dark nothingness. Now I see why it is false to say that a religious person should find death easy and acceptable. Now I understand why it is wrong to think that a death without struggle and agony is a sign of great faith. These ideas do not make much sense once we realize that faith opens us to the full affirmation of life and gives us an intense desire to live more fully, more vibrantly, and more vigorously. If anyone should protest against death it is the religious person, the person who has increasingly come to know God as the God of the living.

This brings me back to the great mystery of today, the day we call Good Friday. It is the day on which Jesus, the Son of God, light of light, true God of true God, one in being with the Father, died. Indeed, on that Friday nearly two thousand years ago, outside the walls of Jerusalem, God died.

I hope you can feel with me that here lies the source of our consolation and hope. God himself, who is light, life, and truth, came to experience with us and for us the total absurdity of death. Jesus' death is not a memorable event because a good, holy prophet died. No, what makes the death of Jesus the main – and in a sense the only real – event in history is that the Son of God, in whom there was no trace of death, died the absurd death that is the fate of all human beings.

This gives us some idea of the agony of Jesus. Who has tasted life more fully than He? Who has known more intimately the beauty of the land in which He lived? Who has understood better the smiles of children, the cries of the sick, and the tears of those in grief? Every fibre of His being spoke of life. 'I am the Way, the Truth and the Life,' He said, and in Him only life could be found. How will we ever be able to grasp what it must have meant for Him to undergo death, to be cut off from life and to enter into the darkness of total destruction! The agony in the garden, the humiliation of the mockery, the pains of the flagellation, the sorrowful way to Calvary, and the horrendous execution on the Cross were suffered by the Lord of life.

I write this to you not to upset you but to console you in your grief. The Lord who died, died for us – for you, for me, for mother, and for all people. He died not because of any death or darkness in Him, but only to free us from the death and darkness in us. If the God who revealed life to us, and whose only desire is to bring us to life, loved us so much that He wanted to experience with us the total absurdity of death, then – yes, then there must be hope; then there must be something more than death; then there must be a promise that is not fulfilled in our short existence in this world; then leaving behind the ones you love, the flowers and the trees, the mountains and the oceans, the beauty of art and music, and all the exuberant gifts of life cannot be just the destruction and cruel end of all things; then indeed we have to wait for the third day.

8

I am looking at the photograph you took of mother's grave. I look at the simple light brown wooden cross. The two heavy beams speak of strength. I read the words 'In Peace', her name,

'Maria', and the dates of her birth and death. They summarize it all. It is a lovely picture. What an exuberance of flowers! They really are splendid. With their white, yellow, red and purple colours, they seem to lift up the cross and speak of life. Oh, how well I remember the 14th of October, six months ago today. What a beautiful morning that was! How gently the sun's rays covered the land when we carried her to this place! Do you remember? It was a sad day, but not only sad. There was a feeling of fulfilment, too. Her life had come to its fulfilment, and it had been such a gracious life. And there was gratitude in our hearts for her and for all who came to tell us what she had meant to them. It was a peaceful, quiet and intimate day. I know you will never forget that day. Neither will I. It was the day that gave us strength to live on in quiet joy, not only looking backward but also forward.

Every time I look at that photograph of her grave, I experience again the new emotion that came to me after we buried her, an emotion so different from the emotion of seeing her again after a long absence, so different too from the emotion of watching her suffer and die. It is a new, very precious emotion. It is the emotion of a quiet, joyful waiting. Surely you know what I mean. There is a quiet contentment in this emotion. She has finished her life with us. She no longer has to suffer as we do; she no longer has to worry as we do; she no longer has to face the fear of death as we do. More than that, she will be spared the many anxieties and conflicts we still have to face. Nobody can harm her any more. We no longer have to protect her and be concerned about her health and safety. Oh, how we should love to have that concern again! But we have laid her to rest and she will not return. The rich soil in which we have buried her, the green hedges behind her grave, and the high lush trees around the small cemetery all create a feeling of safety, of being well received. But there is another side to this emotion. It includes waiting, quiet waiting. The solid, simple cross that stands above her grave speaks of something more than her death. Every time we go to that place, we sense that we are waiting, expecting, hoping. We wish to see her again and be with her once more, but we know that she has left us not to come back. At times, we wish to die and join her in death, but we know that we are called to live and to work on this earth. Our quiet, joyful waiting is much deeper than wishful thinking. It is waiting with the knowledge that love is stronger than death and that this truth will become visible to us. How? When? Where? These questions keep rushing into our impatient hearts. And yet, when we experience that quiet, joyful waiting, they cease troubling us and we feel that all is well.

You may have guessed, dear father, that I am writing this part to you on Holy Saturday. I have lived through this day many times, but this Saturday, April 14, 1979, is unique because today I have a new insight into what the quiet silence of this day means.

You know the story. They had laid Him in the tomb that was in the garden close to the place where He was crucified. Joseph of Arimathea 'rolled a stone against the entrance to the tomb' and 'Mary of Magdala and Mary the mother of Joset were watching and took note of where he was laid.' 'Then they returned and prepared spices and ointments. And on the sabbath day they rested.'

This is the quietest day of the year: no work, no great liturgical celebration, no visitors, no mail, no words. Just a very, very deep repose. A silent, in-between time. Lent is over but Easter has not yet come. He died, but we do not yet fully know what that means. The anxious, fearful tension of Good Friday is gone but no bells have yet been heard. A brother calls me to prayer with a wooden clapper. It has stopped raining. The raging storm that came over the valley last night has withdrawn, but clouds still cover the sky. Yes, a silent, joyful waiting. No panic, no despair, no screams, no tears or wringing of hands. No shouts of joy, either. No victorious songs, no banners or flags. Only a simple, quiet waiting with the deep, inner knowledge that all will be well. How? Do not ask. Why? Do not worry. Where? You will know. When? Just wait. Just wait quietly, peacefully, joyfully … all will be well.

Sacred Saturday! The day on which we buried mother; the day on which we sit near Jesus' tomb and rest; the day on which monks look at each other as if they know something about which they are not yet allowed to speak. It is the day when I understand what your life has been like since you laid mother in her grave.

Do you feel what I am writing about? There are many, many questions, and we would like answers to them now. But it is too early. Nobody knows what to say. We saw that death is real. We saw that death took away from us the one we loved most. We stand by the grave. Let us not ask questions now. This is the time to let that inner quietude grow in us. The disciples thought that it was all over, finished, come to an end … if they thought much at all. The women wanted to take care of the grave. They prepared spices and ointments. But on Saturday, they all rested.

Doesn't this Holy Saturday give us a new insight into what our new life without mother can increasingly become? Doesn't this Holy Saturday tell us about this new emotion of quiet, joyful waiting in which we can grow steadily and securely? No longer do we have to cry; no longer do we have to feel the painful tearing away. Now we can wait, silencing all our wishes and fantasies about what will be, and simply hope in joy.

9

After I began to write this letter to you something happened that at first seemed rather insignificant to me. In the days following, however, it took on more and more importance. Therefore, I want to tell you about it before I finish this letter. It is a weather story. The weather here in upstate New York was lovely up until ten days ago. The winter was over, the spring had begun. The climate was mild and sunny, and the monks enjoyed walking through the woods and observing the first signs of the new season. Yellow, white and blue crocuses decorated the yard, and everybody seemed happy that another cold season had come to an end. But not so! On the day I finally got myself organized enough to begin writing you this letter, a violent storm broke over the land, bringing with it heavy rains. Buckets appeared under the leaks in the roof, windows were shut securely, and no one ventured forth from the house. The temperature dropped sharply, and soon the rain turned into snow. The next day we were back in winter. It kept snowing the whole day, and I felt strangely disoriented. My whole body had been anticipating bright flowers, green trees, and songbirds, and this strange new weather felt totally incongruous. When the storm was over, the landscape seemed idyllic, like a Christmas card. The snow was fresh and beautiful and had settled on the green fields and fir trees like a fresh white robe. But I could not enjoy it. I simply kept saying to myself, 'Well, one week from now it will be Easter and then it will be spring again.' I discovered in myself a strange certainty that Easter would change the weather. And when everything was still pure white on Wednesday of Holy Week, I continued to feel, 'Only three more days and everything will be green again!' Well, on Good Friday stormy winds rose up, a miserable rain began to come down, and it poured for the rest of the day. The next morning all the snow was gone. In the afternoon the clouds dissolved and a brilliant sun appeared, transforming everything into a joyous spectacle. When I looked out of my window and saw the fresh, clear light covering the meadows, I had a hard time not breaking the monastic silence! I walked out and went up to the ridge from which I could overlook the valley. I just smiled and smiled. And I spoke out loudly to the skies, 'The Lord is risen; He is risen indeed!'

Never in my life have I sensed so deeply that the sacred events that we celebrate affect our natural surroundings. It was much more than the feeling of a happy coincidence. It was the intense realization that the events we were celebrating were the real events and that everything else, nature and culture included, was dependent on these events.

You will probably want to know now what the weather was like on Easter morning. It was gentle and cloudy. Nothing very unusual. No rain, no wind; not very cold, not very warm. No radiant sun, only a gentle, soft breeze. It did not really matter much to me. I would probably have been happy even if there had been snow again. What mattered to me was that I had come to experience during this holy season that the real events are the events that take place under the great veil of nature and history. All depends on whether we have eyes that see and ears that hear.

This is what I so much want to write to you on this Easter of 1979. Something very deep and mysterious, very holy and sacred, is taking place in our lives right where we are, and the more attentive we become the more we will begin to see and hear it. The more our spiritual sensitivities come to the surface of our daily lives, the more we will discover – uncover – a new presence in our lives. I have a strong sense that mother's death has been, and still is, a painful but very blessed purification that will enable us to hear a voice and see a face we had not seen or heard as clearly before.

Think of what is happening at Easter. A group of women go to the tomb, notice that the stone has been moved away, enter, see a young man in a white robe sitting on the righthand side, and hear him say, 'He is not here.' Peter and John come running to the tomb and find it empty. Mary of Magdala meets a gardener who calls her by name, and she realizes it is Jesus. The disciples, anxiously huddled together in a closed room, suddenly find Him standing among them and hear Him say, 'Peace be with you.' Two men come hurrying back from Emmaus and tell their puzzled friends that they met Jesus on the road and recognized Him in the breaking of the bread. Later on, Simon Peter, Thomas, Nathanael, James and John are fishing on the lake. A man on the shore calls to them, 'Have you caught anything, friends?' They call back, 'No.' Then He says, 'Throw the net out to starboard and you'll find something.' They do, and when they catch so many fish that they cannot haul in their net, John says to Peter, 'It is the Lord.' And as these events are taking place, a new word is being spoken, at first softly and hesitatingly, then clearly and convincingly, and finally loudly and triumphantly, 'The Lord is risen; He is risen indeed!'

I wonder how this story, the most important story of human history, speaks to you now that you know so well what it means to have lost the one you loved most. Have you noticed that none of the friends of Jesus, neither the women nor the disciples, had the faintest expectation of His return from death? His crucifixion had crushed all their hopes and expectations, and they felt totally lost and dejected. Even when Jesus appeared to them, they kept hesitating and doubting and needing to be convinced, not only Thomas but others as well. There was no trace of an 'I-always-told-you-so' attitude. The event of Jesus' resurrection totally and absolutely surpassed their understanding. It went far beyond their own ways of thinking and feeling. It broke through the limits of their minds and hearts. And still, they believed – and their faith changed the world.

Isn't this good news? Doesn't this turn everything around and offer us a basis on which we can live with hope? Doesn't this put mother's death in a completely new perspective? It does not make her death less painful or our own grief less heavy. It does not make the loss of her less real, but it makes us see and feel that death is part of a much greater and much deeper event, the fullness of which we cannot comprehend, but of which we know that it is a life-bringing event. The friends of Jesus saw Him and heard Him only a few times after that Easter morning, but their lives were completely changed. What seemed to be the end proved to be the beginning; what seemed to be a cause for fear proved to be a cause for courage; what seemed to be defeat proved to be victory; and what seemed to be the basis for despair proved to be the basis for hope. Suddenly a wall becomes a gate, and although we are not able to say with much clarity or precision what lies beyond that gate, the tone of all that we do and say on our way to the gate changes drastically.

The best way I can express to you the meaning death receives in the light of the resurrection of Jesus is to say that the love that causes us so much grief and makes us feel so fully the absurdity of death is stronger than death itself. 'Love is stronger than death.' This sentence summarizes better than any other the meaning of the resurrection and therefore also the meaning of death. I have mentioned this earlier in this letter, but now you may better see its full meaning. Why has mother's death caused you so much suffering? Because you loved her so much. Why has your own death become such an urgent question for you? Because you love life, you love your children and your grandchildren, you love nature, you love art and music, you love horses, and you love all that is alive and beautiful. Death is absurd and cannot be meaningful for someone who loves so much.

The resurrection of Jesus Christ is the glorious manifestation of the victory of love over death. The same love that makes us mourn and protest against death will now free us to live in hope. Do you realize that Jesus appeared only to those who knew Him, who had listened to His words and who had come to love him deeply? It was that love that gave them the eyes to see His face and the ears to hear His voice when he appeared to them on the third day after His death. Once they had seen and heard Him and believed, the rest of their lives became a continuing recognition of His presence in their midst. This is what life in the Spirit of the risen Christ is all about. It makes us see that under the veil of all that is visible to our bodily eyes, the risen Lord shows us His inexhaustible love and calls us to enter even more fully into that love, a love that embraces both mother and us, who loved her so much.

It is with this divine love in our hearts, a love stronger than death, that our lives can be lived as a promise. Because this great love promises us that what we have already begun to see and hear with the eyes and ears of the Spirit of Christ can never be destroyed, but rather is 'the beginning' of eternal life.

Today is the third day of Easter. Easter Tuesday. Here in the Trappist monastery it is the last day of the Easter festivities. For three days we have celebrated the resurrection of Jesus Christ, and it has been a real feast. Although the monks speak with each other only when necessary, and although there are no parties or parades, the Easter days have been more joyful than any I have celebrated in the past. The liturgies have been rich and exuberant with their many alleluias; the readings have been joyful and affirmative; the music has been festive; and everyone has been filled with gratitude towards God and each other.

On Easter Sunday I read the Gospel story about Peter and John running to the tomb and finding it empty. There were more than a hundred visitors in the abbey church, some from far away and some from nearby, some young and some old, some formally and some casually dressed. Sitting with forty monks around the huge rock that serves as the altar, they gave me a real sense of the Church. After reading the Gospel, I preached. I had seldom preached on Easter Sunday during my twenty-two years of priesthood, and I felt very grateful that I could announce to all who were present: 'The Lord is risen; He is risen indeed.' Everyone listened with great attention and I had a sense that the risen Christ was really among us, bringing us His peace. During the Eucharist, I prayed for you, for mother, and for all who are dear to us. I felt that the risen Christ brought us all together, bridging not only the distance between Holland and the United States but also that between life and death. Lent was long, sometimes very hard, and not without its dark moments and tempting demons. But now, in the light of the resurrection of Christ, Lent seems to have been short and easy. I guess this is true for all of life. In darkness we doubt that there will ever be light, but in the light we soon forget how much darkness there was.

Now there is light. In fact, the sun has even broken through and the large stretches of blue sky now visible behind the clusters of clouds remind me again that often what we see is not what is most enduring.

Dear father, this seems the most natural time to conclude not only the Easter celebration but also this letter. For twelve days I have been reflecting on mother's death in the hope of offering you and myself some comfort and consolation. I do not know if I have been able to reach you in your loneliness and grief. Maybe my words often said more to me than to you. But even if this is so, I still hope that the simple fact that these words have been written by your son about her whom we have both loved so much will be a source of consolation to you.

THE LIVING REMINDER

To the alumni of Yale Divinity School
whose continuing interest and support
is a source of great encouragement for
its students and faculty.

Contents

Acknowledgments

The content of this book was first presented in the form of three lectures at the International Conference of the Association for Clinical Pastoral Education and the Canadian Association for Pastoral Education.

I am grateful to Vernon Kuehn for inviting me to the conference and to Robert Bilheimer, director of the Institute for Ecumenical and Cultural Research in Collegeville, Minnesota, for offering me a quiet place, a peaceful time, and a gentle community in which to work. I also want to thank Fred Hofheinz and the staff of the Lilly Endowment for the encouragement and financial support.

I owe a special word of thanks to Jack Jerome, Jim Mason and Bud Kaicher for their skilful typing of the manuscript, to Phil Zaeder for his sound advice, and to Sylvia Zaeder and Stephen Leahy for their editorial assistance.

Finally, I want to express my deep appreciation to my friend and assistant John Mogabgab whose many insights and suggestions helped me to give this book its final form.

Prologue
Exploring Connections

What are the spiritual resources of ministers? What prevents them from becoming dull, sullen, luke-warm bureaucrats, people who have many projects, plans and appointments but who have lost their heart somewhere in the midst of their activities? What keeps ministers vital, alive, energetic and full of zeal? What allows them to preach and teach, counsel and celebrate with a continuing sense of wonder, joy, gratitude and praise?

These are the questions of this book. They concern the relationship between the professional and the personal life of those who want to work in the service of the Gospel. They call for a careful exploration of the connections between ministry and spirituality.

Ministry is service in the name of the Lord. It is bringing the good news to the poor, proclaiming liberty to captives and new sight to the blind, setting the downtrodden free and announcing the Lord's year of favour (Luke 4:18). Spirituality is attention to the life of the spirit in us; it is going out to the desert or up to the mountain to pray; it is standing before the Lord with open heart and open mind; it is crying out, 'Abba, Father'; it is contemplating the unspeakable beauty of our loving God.

We have fallen into the temptation of separating ministry from spirituality, service from prayer. Our demon says: 'We are too busy to pray; we have too many needs to attend to, too many people to respond to, too many wounds to heal. Prayer is a luxury, something to do during a free hour, a day away from work or on a retreat. The few who are exclusively concerned with prayer – such as Trappists, Poor Clares, and some isolated hermits – are really not involved in ministry. They are set free for single-minded contemplation and leave Christian service to others.' But to think this way is harmful; harmful for ministers as well as for contemplatives. Service and prayer can never be separated; they are related to each other as the Yin and Yang of the Japanese Circle.

In this book I want to explore the connection between ministry and spirituality and show how service is prayer and prayer is service. After considerable thought, I felt that the best way to set about this exploration would be to look at ministry as 'remembrance' and at the minister as a living reminder of Jesus Christ. In both the Old and New Testament 'to remember' has a central place. Abraham Joshua Heschel says: 'Much of what the Bible demands can be comprised in one word, "Remember."'[1] And Nihls Dahl, speaking about early Christianity, says: 'The first obligation of the apostle vis-à-vis the community – beyond founding it – is to make the faithful remember what they have received and already know – or should know.'[2] So it is in keeping with the core of the biblical tradition to look at ministry in the context of remembrance. Therefore, I will discuss our spiritual resources by looking at the minister as a reminder: first, as a healing reminder, second as a sustaining reminder, third as a guiding reminder. The terms healing, sustaining, and guiding have been discussed in a masterful way by Seward Hiltner in his

[1] Abraham Joshua Heschel, *Man is not Alone* (New York: Farrar, Straus & Giroux, 1951), p. 161.
[2] Nihls Dahl, 'Anamnesis: Memory and Commemoration in Early Christianity,' *Studia Theologica*, 1 (1947), p. 75.

Preface to Pastoral Theology.[3] In the following three chapters I would like to use the same terms to express my great indebtedness to Seward Hiltner as my teacher and to share my conviction that spiritual resources can be sought and found in the heart of our ministry. Moreover, these terms will help to establish a connection between our present-day concerns with the spiritual life and the many new insights into interpersonal relationships that we have received from the social sciences in recent decades and incorporated into the practice of the ministry.

[3] Seward Hiltner, *Preface to Pastoral Theology* (New York: Abingdon Press, 1954).

The Minister as a
Healing Reminder

INTRODUCTION

Let me start with a story about Elie Wiesel. In 1944, all the Jews
of the Hungarian town of Sighet were rounded up and deported
to concentration camps. Elie Wiesel, the now famous novelist,
was one of them. He survived the holocaust and twenty years
later returned to see his home town again. What pained him
most was that the people of Sighet had erased the Jews from
their memory. He writes:

> I was not angry with the people of Sighet ... for having driven
> out their neighbours of yesterday, nor for having denied them.
> If I was angry at all it was for having forgotten them. So quic-
> kly, so completely ... Jews have been driven not only out of
> town but out of time as well.[1]

This story suggests that to forget our sins may be an even greater
sin than to commit them. Why? Because what is forgotten cannot be healed and that which cannot be healed easily becomes
the cause of greater evil. In his many books about the holocaust,

---

[1] Elie Wiesel, *Legends of Our Time* (New York: Holt, Rinehart and Winston,
 1968), pp. 123, 128.

Elie Wiesel does not remind us of Auschwitz, Buchenwald and Treblinka to torture our consciences with heightened guilt feelings, but to allow our memories to be healed and so to prevent an even worse disaster. An Auschwitz that is forgotten causes a Hiroshima, and a forgotten Hiroshima can cause the destruction of our world. By cutting off our past we paralyse our future: forgetting the evil behind us we evoke the evil in front of us. As George Santayana has said: 'He who forgets the past is doomed to repeat it.'

With this in mind I would like to discuss how the minister as a reminder is first of all a healer who, by healing our wounded past, can open up a new future. I will touch on three areas: the wounds, the healing and the healer.

THE WOUNDS

The French writer-politician André Malraux writes in his *Anti-Memoirs*, 'One day it will be realized that men are distinguishable from one another as much by the forms their memories take as by their characters.'[2] This is a very important observation. The older we grow the more we have to remember, and at some point we realize that most, if not all, of what we have is memory. Our memory plays a central role in our sense of being. Our pains and joys, our feelings of grief and satisfaction, are not simply dependent on the events of our lives, but also, and even more so, on the ways we remember these events. The events of our lives are probably less important than the form they take in the totality of our story. Different people remember a similar illness, accident, success or surprise in very different ways, and much of their sense of self derives less from what happened

---

[2] André Malraux, *Anti-Memoirs* (New York: Bantam Books, 1970), p. 125.

than from how they remember what happened, how they have placed the past events into their own personal history.

It is not surprising, therefore, that most of our human emotions are closely related to our memory. Remorse is a biting memory, guilt is an accusing memory, gratitude is a joyful memory, and all such emotions are deeply influenced by the way we have integrated past events into our way of being in the world. In fact, we perceive our world with our memories. Our memories help us to see and understand new impressions and give them a place in our richly varied life experiences.

I have always been fascinated by the way immigrants, especially Dutchmen, respond to the USA when they come here for the first time. The first way they make themselves feel at home in their new country is to look at things which remind them of the old country. Then they start to see all the things which are larger, bigger, wider and heavier than at home. Finally, often after several years, they begin to compare things within the country: the East with the West, the city with the countryside. When that happens then they are at home. Then they have built up a large enough store of memories in the USA to compare its different parts and aspects.

These observations show how crucial our memory is for the way we experience life. This is why, in all helping professions – such as medicine, psychiatry, psychology, social work – the first questions are always directed to the memory of the patient or client. 'Please tell me your story. What brought you here? What are the events which led you to this place here and now?' And it is clear that what doctors and therapists hear about are not just events but memories of events.

It is no exaggeration to say that the suffering we most frequently encounter in the ministry is a suffering of memories. They are the wounding memories that ask for healing. Feelings of alienation, loneliness, separation; feelings of anxiety, fear,

suspicion; and related symptoms such as nervousness, sleepless-
ness, nail-biting – these all are part of the forms which certain
memories have taken. These memories wound because they are
often deeply hidden in the centre of our being and very hard to
reach. While the good memories may be present to us in outer
signs such as trophies, decorations, diplomas, precious stones,
vases, rings and portraits, painful memories tend to remain
hidden from us in the corner of our forgetfulness. It is from
this hidden place that they escape healing and cause so much
harm.

Our first and most spontaneous response to our undesirable
memories is to forget them. When something painful has happened we quickly say to ourselves and to each other: 'Let's forget it, let's act as if it did not happen, let's not talk about it, let's
think about happier things.' We want to forget the pains of the
past – our personal, communal and national traumas – and live
as if they did not really happen. But by not remembering them
we allow the forgotten memories to become independent forces
that can exert a crippling effect on our functioning as human
beings. When this happens, we become strangers to ourselves
because we cut down our own history to a pleasant, comfortable
size and try to make it conform to our own daydreams.
Forgetting the past is like turning our most intimate teacher
against us. By refusing to face our painful memories we miss the
opportunity to change our hearts and grow mature in repentance. When Jesus says, 'It is not the healthy who need the doctor, but the sick' (Mark 2:17), he affirms that only those who
face their wounded condition can be available for healing and
so enter into a new way of living.

THE HEALING

How are we healed of our wounding memories? We are healed first of all by letting them be available, by leading them out of the corner of forgetfulness and by remembering them as part of our life stories. What is forgotten is unavailable, and what is unavailable cannot be healed. Max Scheler shows how memory liberates us from the determining power of forgotten painful events. 'Remembering,' he says, 'is the beginning of freedom from the covert power of the remembered thing or occurrence.'[3]

If ministers are reminders, their first task is to offer the space in which the wounding memories of the past can be reached and brought back into the light without fear. When the soil is not ploughed the rain cannot reach the seeds; when the leaves are not raked away the sun cannot nurture the hidden plants. So also, when our memories remain covered with fear, anxiety, or suspicion the word of God cannot bear fruit.

To be a reminder requires a dynamic understanding of the lives and behaviour of those who need to be reminded, an understanding which offers insight into the many psychic forces by which painful memories are rejected. Anton Boisen, the father of the Movement for Clinical Pastoral Education, pleaded for this dynamic understanding when he proposed a 'theology through living human documents'. Many pastoral theologians and psychologists have deepened this understanding with the help and inspiration of the contemporary behavioural sciences.

During the past few decades theological educators have become increasingly convinced of the importance of this dynamic approach to ministry, and the many centres for Clinical Pastoral Education have made great contributions in

[3] Max Scheler, *On the Eternal in Man*, trans. Bernard Noble (New York: Harper and Brothers, 1960), p. 41.

this direction. But today, in the seventies, new questions are being heard. Has the great emphasis on the complex psychodynamics of human behaviour not created a situation in which ministers have become more interested in the receiver of the message than in the message itself? Have we not become more immersed in the language of the behavioural sciences than in the language of the Bible? Are we not talking more about people than about God, in whose name we come to people? Do we not feel closer to the psychologist and psychiatrist than to the priest? Sometimes these questions have an accusatory and self-righteous tone, but often they are raised with an honest desire to move forward with a full appreciation of what has been learned. Such questions challenge us to look beyond the task of accepting. Accepting is only one aspect of the process of healing. The other aspect is connecting.

The great vocation of the minister is to continuously make connections between the human story and the divine story. We have inherited a story which needs to be told in such a way that the many painful wounds about which we hear day after day can be liberated from their isolation and be revealed as part of God's relationship with us. Healing means revealing that our human wounds are most intimately connected with the suffering of God himself. To be a living memory of Jesus Christ, therefore, means to reveal the connections between our small sufferings and the great story of God's suffering in Jesus Christ, between our little life and the great life of God with us. By lifting our painful forgotten memories out of the egocentric, individualistic, private sphere, Jesus Christ heals our pains. He connects them with the pain of all humanity, a pain he took upon himself and transformed. To heal, then, does not primarily mean to take pains away but to reveal that our pains are part of a greater pain, that our sorrows are part of a greater sorrow, that our experience is part of the great experience of him who said, 'But was it not ordained that the Christ should suffer and so enter into the glory of God?' (cf. Luke 24:26).

By connecting the human story with the story of the suffering servant, we rescue our history from its fatalistic chain and allow our time to be converted from *chronos* into *kairos*, from a series of randomly organized incidents and accidents into a constant opportunity to explore God's work in our lives. We find a beautiful example revealing this connection in Martin Luther's letter of counsel to Elector Frederick of Saxony. He writes:

> When, therefore, I learned, most illustrious prince, that Your Lordship has been afflicted with a grave illness and that Christ has at the same time become ill in you, I counted it my duty to visit Your Lordship with a little writing of mine. I cannot pretend that I do not hear the voice of Christ crying out to me from Your Lordship's body and flesh and saying: 'Behold I am sick.' This is so because such evils as illness and the like, are not borne by us who are Christian, but by Christ himself, our Lord and Saviour, in whom we live ...[4]

All of ministry rests on the conviction that nothing, absolutely nothing, in our lives is outside the realm of God's judgment and mercy. By hiding parts of our story, not only from our own consciousness but also from God's eye, we claim a divine role for ourselves; we become judges of our own past and limit mercy to our own fears. Thus we disconnect ourselves not only from our own suffering but also from God's suffering for us. The challenge of ministry is to help people in very concrete situations – people with illnesses or in grief, people with physical or mental

---

[4] Martin Luther, *Letters of Spiritual Counsel*, ed. and trans. Theodore G. Tappert, *Library of Christian Classics*, vol. 18 (Philadelphia: The Westminster Press, 1955), p. 27.

handicaps, people suffering from poverty and oppression, people caught in the complex networks of secular or religious institutions – to see and experience their story as part of God's ongoing redemptive work in the world. These insights and experiences heal precisely because they restore the broken connection between the world and God and create a new unity in which memories that formerly seemed only destructive are now reclaimed as part of a redemptive event.

THE HEALER

The minister, as a living memory of God's great deeds in history, is called to heal by reminding people of their wounded past and by connecting their wounds with the wounds of all humanity, redeemed by the suffering of God in Christ. But what are the implications of such a viewpoint for the personal life of the minister? The temptation is strong to ask the 'how' question: 'How do I become a living memory of God; how do I accept and connect; how do I lift up the individual story into the divine history?' These questions are temptations insofar as they avoid the more basic question: 'Who am I as a living memory of God?' The main question indeed is not a question of doing, but a question of being. When we speak about the minister as a living reminder of God, we are not speaking about a technical speciality which can be mastered through the acquisition of specific tools, techniques and skills, but about a way of being which embraces the totality of life: working and resting, eating and drinking, praying and playing, acting and waiting. Before any professional skill, we need a spirituality, a way of living in the spirit by which all we are and all we do becomes a form of reminding.

One way to express this is to say that in order to be a living reminder of the Lord, we must walk in His presence as Abraham did. To walk in the presence of the Lord means to move forward in life in such a way that all our desires, thoughts, and actions are constantly guided by Him. When we walk in the Lord's presence, everything we see, hear, touch, or taste reminds us of Him. This is what is meant by a prayerful life. It is not a life in which we say many prayers, but a life in which nothing, absolutely nothing, is done, said, or understood independently of Him who is the origin and purpose of our existence. This is powerfully expressed by the nineteenth-century Russian Orthodox *staretz*, Theophan the Recluse:

> Into every duty a God-fearing heart must be put, a heart constantly permeated by the thought of God; and this will be the door through which the soul will enter into active life. ... The essence is to be established in the remembrance of God, and to walk in His presence.[5]

Thus Theophan the Recluse stresses that our mind and heart should be exclusively directed to the Lord and that we should see and understand the world in and through Him. This is the challenge of the Christian and especially that of the minister. It is the challenge to break through our most basic alienation and live a life of total connectedness.

The strategy of the principalities and powers is to disconnect us, to cut us off from the memory of God. It is not hard to see how many of our busy actions and restless concerns seem to be disconnected, reminding us of nothing more than the disorder of our own orientation and commitment. When we no longer walk in the presence of the Lord, we cannot be living reminders of His divine presence in our lives. We then quickly become

---

[5] Theophan the Recluse in Igumen Chariton, *The Art of Prayer*, ed. by Timothy Ware (London: Faber and Faber, 1966), pp. 85, 98.

strangers in an alien land who have forgotten where we come from and where we are going. Then we are no longer the way to the experience of God, but rather *in* the way of the experience of God. Then, instead of walking in God's presence we start walking in a vicious circle, and pulling others into it.

At first sight this may seem rather pious and unrealistic, but not for long. The emphasis on ministry as a profession that has dominated our thinking during the past several decades may have led us to put too much confidence in our abilities, skills, techniques, projects and programmes. In so doing, we have lost touch with that reality with which we are called to connect, not so much by what we do, but by who we are.

In recent years I have become more and more aware of my own tendency to think that the value of my presence depends on what I say or do. And yet it is becoming clearer to me every day that this preoccupation with performing in fact prevents me from letting God speak through me in any way he wants, and so keeps me from making connections prior to any special word or deed.

In no way am I trying to minimize or even to criticize the importance of training for the ministry. I am simply suggesting that this training will bear more fruit when it occurs in the context of a spirituality, a way of life in which we are primarily concerned, not to be with people but to be with God, not to walk in the presence of anyone who asks for our attention but to walk in the presence of God – a spirituality, in short, which helps us to distinguish service from our need to be liked, praised or respected.

Over the years we have developed the idea that being present to people in all their needs is our greatest and primary vocation. The Bible does not seem to support this. Jesus' primary concern was to be obedient to His Father, to live constantly in His presence. Only then did it become clear to Him what His task was in His relationships with people. This also is the way He proposes for His apostles: 'It is to the glory of my Father that you should bear much fruit and then you will be my disciples' (John 15:8). Perhaps we must continually remind ourselves that the first commandment requiring us to love God with all our heart, all our soul, and all our mind is indeed the first. I wonder if we really belive this. It seems that in fact we live as if we should give as much of our heart, soul and mind as possible to our fellow human beings, while trying hard not to forget God. At least we feel that our attention should be divided evenly between God and our neighbour. But Jesus' claim is much more radical. He asks for a single-minded commitment to God and God alone. God wants all of our heart, all of our mind, and all of our soul. It is this unconditional and unreserved love for God that leads to the care for our neighbour, not as an activity which distracts us from God or competes with our attention to God, but as an expression of our love for God who reveals Himself to us as the God of all people. It is in God that we find our neighbours and discover our responsibility to them. We might even say that only in God does our neighbour become a neighbour rather than an infringement upon our autonomy, and that only in and through God does service become possible.

At first this may appear to contradict the widely shared perspective which maintains that we come to know God only through relationships with our neighbours, and that service to the neighbour is also service to God (cf. Matt. 24:34–40). This viewpoint is firmly rooted in our personal experience and so has an immediacy which is convincing. And it is indeed true that God may meet us in the neighbour. But it is crucial for our ministry that we not confuse our relationship with God with our relationships with our neighbours. It is because God first loved us that we can love our neighbours rather than demand things of them. The first commandment receives concreteness and specificity through the second; the second commandment becomes possible through the first. The first and second commandment should never be separated or made mutually exclusive, neither should they be confused or substituted one for the other. That is why the second commandment is equal to the first, and that is why all ministry is based on our personal and communal relationship with God. This is what Dietrich Bonhoeffer says in his books, *The Communion of Saints* and *The Cost of Discipleship*. It is also the core idea of Thomas Merton's writings, and it was the intuition of all the great Christian leaders, who considered a growing intimacy with Christ the source of all their actions.

And so, to be living reminders of God we must be concerned first of all with our own intimacy with God. Once we have heard, seen, watched, and touched the Word who is life, we cannot do other than be living reminders. Once our lives are connected with His, we will speak about Him, sing His praise, and proclaim His great deeds, not out of obligation but as a free, spontaneous response. In order for this response to be lasting and oriented to the felt needs of those to whom we minister, we need discipline, formation and training. But these can do little more than offer channels for the lived experience of God.

CONCLUSION

In this discussion of the minister as a healing reminder, I have stressed three points. First of all, ministers heal by reminding. Second, they remind by accepting the wounds of our individual pasts and by connecting them with the wounds of all humanity suffered by God Himself. Finally, this reminding happens not so much because of what ministers say or do but by how their own lives are intimately connected with God in Jesus Christ. This means that to be a healing reminder requires a spirituality, a spiritual connectedness, a way of living united with God. What does this imply for the daily life of the minister?

It implies that prayer, not in the sense of *prayers*, but in the sense of a prayerful life, a life lived in connection with Christ should be our first and overriding concern.

It implies that in a life of connectedness with Christ the needs of our neighbours and the nature of our service are disclosed.

It implies that all training and formation are intended to facilitate this disclosure, and that the insights of the behavioural sciences should be seen as aids in this process.

It implies that prayer cannot be considered external to the process of ministry. If we heal by reminding each other of God in Christ, then we must have the mind of Christ Himself to do so. For that, prayer is indispensable.

Finally, it implies that what counts is not our lives, but the life of Christ in us. Ultimately, it is Christ in us from whom healing comes. Only Christ can break through our human alienation and restore the broken connections with each other and with God.

The Minister as a
Sustaining Reminder

INTRODUCTION

Let me start again with Elie Wiesel. In *The Town Beyond the Wall*[1] and *A Beggar in Jerusalem*,[2] Wiesel evokes in a masterful way the sustaining power of friendship. In both books it is not simply from a friend but from the memory of a friend that the sustaining power flows.

In *The Town Beyond the Wall* it is Michael who lives through torture but avoids madness because Pedro, his absent friend, lives in his memory and so sustains him in the midst of his agony. And in *A Beggar in Jerusalem* it is David who is sustained in his struggles by the memory of his friend Katriel, killed during Israel's Six-Day War. This is a crucial theme in Wiesel's writings. He wants us to remember not only the wounds but also the great affectionate bonds of our life stories. Just as the memory of past wounds can prevent us from repeating the evil that wounded us, so also the memory of love can nurture us in our day-to-day struggles. In his novels Wiesel expresses the profound truth that memory not only connects us with our past but also keeps us alive in the present. He touches here a mystery deeply

[1] Elie Wiesel, *The Town Beyond the Wall* (New York: Atheneum, 1964).
[2] Elie Wiesel, *A Beggar in Jerusalem* (New York: Random House, 1970).

anchored in the biblical tradition. When Israel remembers God's great acts of love and compassion, she enters into these great acts themselves. To remember is not simply to look back at past events; more importantly, it is to bring these events into the present and celebrate them here and now. For Israel, remembrance means participation. Brevard S. Childs writes: 'The act of remembering serves to actualize the past for a generation removed in time from those former events in order that they themselves can have an intimate encounter with the great acts of redemption … Although separated in time and space from the sphere of God's revelation in the past, through memory the gulf is spanned, and the exiled people share again in redemptive history.'[3]

It is central to the biblical tradition that God's love for His people should not be forgotten. It should remain with us in the present. When everything is dark, when we are surrounded by despairing voices, when we do not see any exits, then we can find salvation in a remembered love, a love which is not simply a wistful recollection of a bygone past but a living force which sustains us in the present. Through memory, love transcends the limits of time and offers hope at any moment of our lives.

This is the message of the Bible. This is the message which Elie Wiesel puts in the context of the agonies of our century. This also is the message which forms the core of our lives as ministers of the Gospel of Jesus Christ. Therefore, I will speak now about the minister as a sustaining reminder. Again, three aspects present themselves to us: the sustenance, the sustaining, and the sustainer.

[3] Brevard S. Childs, *Memory and Tradition in Israel* (London: SCM Press, 1962), pp. 56, 60.

THE SUSTENANCE

One of the mysteries of life is that memory can often bring us closer to each other than can physical presence. Physical presence not only invites but also blocks intimate communication. In our preresurrection state our bodies hide as much as they reveal. Indeed, many of our disappointments and frustrations in life are related to the fact that seeing and touching each other does not always create the closeness we seek. The more experience in living we have, the more we sense that closeness grows in the continuous interplay between presence and absence.

In absence, from a distance, in memory, we see each other in a new way. We are less distracted by each other's idiosyncracies and are better able to see and understand each other's inner core.

When I am away from home, I often express myself in letters in a much more intimate way than when I am with my family. And when I am away from school, students often write letters in which they say things they were never able to express when I was around.

In memory we are able to be in touch with each other's spirit, with that reality in each other which enables an always deepening communication. There is little doubt that memory can distort, falsify, and cause selective perception. But that is only one aspect of memory. Memory also clarifies, purifies, brings into focus, and calls to the foreground hidden gifts. When a mother and father think of their children who have left home, when a child remembers his parents, when a husband and wife call each other to mind during long periods of absence, when friends recall their friends, it is often the very best that is evoked and the real beauty of the other that breaks through into consciousness. When we remember each other with love we evoke each other's spirit and so enter into a new intimacy, a spiritual union with each other. At the same time, however, the loving memory always makes us desire to be in touch again, to see each other anew, to return to the shared life where the newly found spirit can become more concretely expressed and more deeply embedded in the mutuality of love. But a deeper presence always leads again to a more purifying absence. Thus the continuous interplay between presence and absence, linked by our creative memory, is the way in which our love for each other is purified, deepened and sustained.

This sustaining power of memory becomes most mysteriously visible in God's revelation in Jesus Christ. Indeed it is in memory that we enter into a nurturing and sustaining relationship with Christ. In His farewell discourse Jesus said to His disciples, 'It is for your own good that I am going, because unless I go, the Advocate will not come to you; ... But when the Spirit of truth comes he will lead you to the complete truth' (John 16:7, 13). Here Jesus reveals to His closest friends that only in memory will real intimacy with Him be possible, that only in memory will they experience the full meaning of what they have witnessed.

They listened to His words, they saw Him on Mount Tabor, they heard Him speak about His death and resurrection, but their ears and eyes remained closed and they did not understand. The Spirit, His spirit, had not yet come, and although they saw and heard, smelled and touched Him, they remained distant. Only later when He was gone could His true Spirit reveal itself to them. In His absence a new and more intimate presence became possible, a presence which nurtured and sustained in the midst of tribulations and which created the desire to see Him again. The great mystery of the divine revelation is that God entered into intimacy with us not only by Christ's coming, but also by His leaving. Indeed, it is in Christ's absence that our intimacy with Him is so profound that we can say He dwells in us, call Him our food and drink, and experience him as the centre of our being.

That this is far from a theoretical idea becomes clear in the lives of people like Dietrich Bonhoeffer and Alfred Delp[4] who, while in Nazi prisons waiting for death, experienced Christ's presence in the midst of his absence. Bonhoeffer writes: 'The God who is with us is the God who forsakes us (Mark 15:34) ... Before God and with God we live without God.'[5] Thus the memory of Jesus Christ is much more than the bringing to mind of past redemptive events. It is a life-giving memory, a memory which sustains and nurtures us here and now and so gives us a real sense of being rooted amidst the many crises of daily life.

THE SUSTAINING

How does a ministry as a sustaining memory of Jesus Christ take shape? From what has been said about the maturing interplay between absence and presence, it is clear that we need to look more closely at the ministry of absence. We are living in a culture and social climate which places a great and positive emphasis on presence. We feel that being present is a value as such, and almost always better than being absent. Being present constitutes much of our occupation as ministers: present to patients and students, at services, at Bible groups, at all sorts of charitable meetings, at

[4] Delp, a Jesuit theologian and commentator on social issues in economic and political life for the periodical *Stimmen der Zeit*, was imprisoned by the Nazis in July, 1944. Tried and sentenced to death the following January, he died on February 2, 1945, two months before Bonhoeffer was executed. Delp's prison writings may be found in the third volume of his collected papers: *Christus und Gegenwart*, vol. 3: *Im Angesicht des Todes* (Frankfort am Main: Verlag Josef Knecht, 1949).

[5] Dietrich Bonhoeffer, *Letters and Papers from Prison*, ed. by Eberhard Bethge (New York: Macmillan and Co., 1972), p. 360.

parties, at dinners, at games – and just present in the streets of our town.

Although this ministry of presence is undoubtedly very meaningful, it always needs to be balanced by a ministry of absence. This is so because it belongs to the essence of a creative ministry constantly to convert the pain of the Lord's absence into a deeper understanding of His presence. But absence can only be converted if it is first of all experienced. Therefore, ministers do not fulfil their whole task when they witness only to God's presence and do not tolerate the experience of His absence. If it is true that ministers are living memories of Jesus Christ, then they must search for ways in which not only their presence but also their absence reminds people of their Lord. This has some concrete implications. It calls for the art of leaving, for the ability to be articulately absent, and most of all for a creative withdrawal. Let me illustrate this with the ministry of visitation and the ministry of the Eucharist.

In our ministry of visitation – hospital visits and home visits – it is essential for patients and parishioners to experience that it is good for them, not only that we come but also that we leave. In this way the memory of our visit can become as important, if not more important, than the visit itself. I am deeply convinced that there is a ministry in which our leaving creates space for God's Spirit and in which, by our absence, God can become present in a new way. There is an enormous difference between an absence after a visit and an absence which is the result of not coming at all. Without a coming there can be no leaving, and without a presence absence is only emptiness and not the way to a greater intimacy with God through the Spirit.

The words of Jesus: 'It is for your good that I leave' should be a part of every pastoral call we make. We have to learn to leave so that the Spirit can come. Then we can indeed be remembered as a living witness of God. This shows the importance of being sensitive to the last words we speak before we leave a room or house; it also puts the possibility of a prayer before leaving into a new light.

Not only in pastoral visits but also, and even more so, in the celebration of the sacraments, we need to be aware of the importance of a ministry of absence. This is very central in the Eucharist. What do we do there? We eat bread, but not enough to take our hunger away; we drink wine, but not enough to take our thirst away; we read from a book, but not enough to take our ignorance away. Around these 'poor signs' we come together and celebrate. What then do we celebrate? The simple signs, which cannot satisfy all our desires, speak first of all of God's absence. He has not yet returned; we are still on the road, still waiting, still hoping, still expecting, still longing. We gather around the table with bread, wine, and a book to remind each other of the promise we have received and so to encourage each other to keep waiting in expectation for His return. But even as we affirm His absence we realize that he already is with us. We say to each other: 'Eat and drink, this is His body and blood. The One we are waiting for is our food and drink and is more present to us than we can be to ourselves. He sustains us on the road, He nurtures us as he nurtured His people in the desert.' Thus, while remembering His promises in His absence we discover and celebrate His presence in our midst.

The great temptation of the ministry is to celebrate only the presence of the Lord while forgetting His absence. Often the minister is most concerned to make people glad and to create an atmosphere of 'I'm OK, you're OK.' But in this way everything gets filled up and there is no empty space left for the affirmation of our basic lack of fulfilment. In this way God's presence is enforced without connection with His absence. Almost inevitably this leads to artificial joy and superficial happiness. It also leads to disillusionment because we forget that it is in

258

memory that the Lord is present. If we deny the pain of His absence we will not be able to taste His sustaining presence either.

Therefore, every time ministers call their people around the table, they call them to experience not only the Lord's presence but His absence as well; they call them to mourning as well as to feasting, to sadness as well as to joy, to longing as well as to satisfaction.

And so the Eucharist is a memorial of the Lord's death and resurrection, a memorial which sustains us here and now. As we are being reminded we are nutured. As we become aware of His absence we discover His presence, and as we realize that He left us we also come to know that He did not leave us alone.

So we see that sustaining calls for a patient and humble attitude, an attitude in which we do not create false gaiety, easy excitement, or hollow optimism. The minister is not called to cheer people up but modestly to remind them that in the midst of pains and tribulations the first sign of the new life can be found and a joy can be experienced which is hidden in the midst of sadness.

Therefore, a sustaining ministry requires the art of creative withdrawal so that in memory God's Spirit can manifest itself and lead to the full truth. Without this withdrawal we are in danger of no longer being the way, but *in* the way; of no longer speaking and acting in His name, but in ours; of no longer pointing to the Lord who sustains, but only to our own distracting personalities. If we speak God's word, we have to make it clear that it is indeed God's word we speak and not our own. If we organize a service, we have to be aware that we cannot organize God but only offer boundaries within which God's presence can be sensed. If we visit, we have to remember that we only come because we are sent. If we accept leadership it can only be honest if it takes the form of service. The more this creative withdrawal becomes a real part of our ministry the more we participate in the leaving of Christ, the good leaving that allows the sustaining Spirit to come.

THE SUSTAINER

What are the implications of the ministry of sustaining for the personal life of the minister? Perhaps we need to reconsider a little our ideas about availability. When absence is a part of our ministry, we have to relativize our view of the value of availability. We ministers may have become so available that there is too much presence and too little absence, too much staying with people and too little leaving them, too much of us and too little of God and His Spirit. It is clear that much of this is connected with a certain illusion of indispensability. This illusion needs to be unmasked.

From all I have said about the minister as a sustaining reminder, it becomes clear that a certain unavailability is essential for the spiritual life of the minister. I am not trying to build a religious argument for a game of golf, a trip to a conference, a cruise to the Caribbean, or a sabbatical. These arguments have been made and they all strike me as quite unconvincing in the midst of our suffering world. No, I would like to make a plea for prayer as the creative way of being unavailable.

How would it sound when the question, 'Can I speak to the minister?' is not answered by 'I am sorry, he has someone in his office', but by 'I am sorry, he is praying.' When someone says, 'The minister is unavailable because this is his day of solitude, this is his day in the hermitage, this is his desert day', could that not be a consoling ministry? What it says is that the minister is unavailable to me, not because he is more available to others, but because he is with God, and God alone – the God who is our God.

My spiritual director at the abbey of the Genesee spent one day a week in a small hermitage on the property of the abbey. I remember that his absence had a comforting effect on me. I missed his presence and still I felt grateful that he spent a whole day with God alone. I felt supported, nourished, and strengthened by the knowledge that God was indeed his only concern, that he brought all the concerns of the people he counselled into his intimate relationship with God, and that while he was absent he was, in fact, closer to me than ever.

When our absence from people means a special presence to God, then that absence becomes a sustaining absence. Jesus continuously left His apostles to enter into prayer with the Father. The more I read the Gospels, the more I am struck with Jesus' single-minded concern with the Father. From the day His parents found him in the Temple, Jesus speaks about His Father as the source of all His words and actions. When He withdraws Himself from the crowd and even from His closest friends, he withdraws to be with the Father. 'In the morning, long before dawn, he got up and left the house, and went off to a lonely place and prayed there' (Mark 1:35). All through His life Jesus considers His relationship with the Father as the centre, beginning and end of His ministry. All He says and does He says and does in the name of the Father. He comes from the Father and returns to the Father, and it is in His Father's house that He wants to prepare a place for us.

It is obvious that Jesus does not maintain His relationship with the Father as a means of fulfilling His ministry. On the contrary, His relationship with the Father is the core of His ministry. Therefore, prayer, days alone with God, or moments of silence, should never be seen or understood as healthy devices to keep in shape, to charge our 'spiritual batteries', or to build up energy for ministry. No, they are all ministry. We minister to our parishioners, patients and students even when we are with God and God alone.

It is in the intimacy with God that we develop a greater intimacy with people and it is in the silence and solitude of prayer that we indeed can touch the heart of the human suffering to which we want to minister.

Do we really believe this? It often seems that our professional busyness has claimed the better part of us. It remains hard for us to leave our people, our job, and the hectic places where we are needed, in order to be with Him from whom all good things come. Still, it is in the silence and solitude of prayer that the minister becomes minister. There we remember that if anything worthwhile happens at all it is God's work and not ours.

Prayer is not a way of being busy with God instead of with people. In fact, it unmasks the illusion of busyness, usefulness, and indispensability. It is a way of being empty and useless in the presence of God and so of proclaiming our basic belief that all is grace and nothing is simply the result of hard work. Indeed, wasting time for God is an act of ministry, because it reminds us and our people that God is free to touch anyone regardless of our well-meant efforts. Prayer as an articulate way of being useless in the face of God brings a smile to all we do and creates humour in the midst of our occupations and preoccupations.

Thinking about my own prayer, I realize how easily I make it into a little seminar with God, during which I want to be useful by reading beautiful prayers, thinking profound thoughts and saying impressive words. I am obviously still worried about the grade! It indeed is a hard discipline to be useless in God's presence and to let Him speak in the silence of my heart. But whenever I become a little useless I know that God is calling me to a new life far beyond the boundaries of my usefulness.

We can say therefore that ministry is first and foremost the sharing of this 'useless' prayer with others. It is from the still point of prayer that we can reach out to others and let the sustaining power of God's presence be known. Indeed, it is there that we become living reminders of Jesus Christ.

CONCLUSION

In our discussion of the minister as a sustaining reminder, three ideas have been dominant. First, we sustain each other in the constant interplay between absence and presence. Second, a sustaining ministry asks ministers to be not only creatively present but creatively absent. Third, a creative absence challenges ministers to develop an ever-growing intimacy with God in prayer and to make that the source of their entire ministry.

This means that to be a sustaining reminder we must make our own the words of Jesus: 'It is for your own good that I am going, because unless I go the Advocate [the Holy Spirit] will not come to you' (John 16:7).

What does all this suggest for our daily lives as ministers?

It suggests that we need to explore not only ways of being present to people but also ways of being absent.

It suggests that in the way we visit, preach and celebrate we must keep struggling with the question of how to be the way, without being *in* the way.

It suggests that prayer can never be considered a private affair. Rather, it belongs to the core of ministry and, therefore, is also subject to education and formation.

It suggests that it is important to look at our daily calendars again and schedule some useless time in the midst of our busy work. We ought to schedule our time with God with the same realism that we schedule our time with people.

Finally, it suggests that amidst so many 'useful' people we should try to keep reminding ourselves of our basic uselessness and so bring a smile and a little humour to all we do.

The Minister as a
Guiding Reminder

INTRODUCTION

The first word belongs again to the great reminder, Elie Wiesel.
In his novel *The Gates of the Forest* Wiesel tells the story of
Gregor. Having survived the holocaust, Gregor finds himself in
Paris, seeking a new future after the horrendous trials of his past.
There, on the advice of a friend and not without reluctance, he
visits the rabbi. When the rabbi asks what Gregor expects of
him, the answer is, 'Make me able to cry.'

> The Rebbe shook his head. 'That is not enough. I shall teach
> you to sing. Grown people don't cry, beggars don't cry ...
> Crying is for children. Are you still a child, and is your life a
> child's dream? No, crying's no use. You must sing.'
>   'And you, Rebbe? What do you expect of me?'
>   'Everything.'
>   And when Gregor started to protest, the Rebbe added,
> 'Jacob wrestled with the angel all night and overcame him.
> But the angel implored him: Let me go, dawn is approaching.
> Jacob let him go; to show his gratitude the angel brought him
> a ladder. Bring me this ladder.'
>   'Which one of us is Jacob?' asked Gregor. 'And which the
> angel?'

'I don't know,' said the Rebbe with a friendly wink. 'Do you?'

Gregor got up and the Rebbe took him to the door. 'Promise to come back,' he said, holding out his hand.

'I'll come back.'

'Will you come to our celebrations?'

'Yes.'[1]

This pastoral visit has much to say. Elie Wiesel, who gives to Gregor many autobiographical traits, expresses in this dialogue his hope in a new future. Beyond tears there is singing, beyond sadness there is celebration, beyond the struggle there is the ladder given in gratitude by an angel. The rabbi is the living reminder of a faithful God. When in the same conversation Gregor asks, 'After what happened to us, how can you believe in God?' the Rabbi responds, 'How can you *not* believe in God after what has happened?'[2] The God who wrestles with us also gives us a ladder to a new future. Wiesel, who does not want us to forget the past, does not want us to lose faith in the future either. Harry James Cargas says of Wiesel: 'He knows that each of us is an inheritor of the entire past while being the beginning point for all the future.'[3] And so Wiesel, the great reminder, becomes a hopeful guide.

There is little doubt that it was the Hasidic tradition with its deep faith in God that enabled Wiesel to speak about hope after the holocaust. During his early youth, Hasidism had impregnated Wiesel's heart, mind, and soul and given him a memory of God which could not be erased, even by the

---

[1] Elie Wiesel, *The Gates of the Forest* (New York: Holt, Rinehart and Winston, 1966), p. 198.

[2] *ibid.*, p. 194.

[3] Harry James Cargas, *In Conversation with Elie Wiesel* (New York: Paulist Press, 1976), pp. 121–122.

holocaust. It proved to be his saving guide in the years of grief and mourning.

Ministers, as living reminders of Jesus Christ, are not only healers and sustainers, but also guides. The memory that heals the wounds of our past and sustains us in the present also guides us to the future and makes our lives continuously new. To be living reminders means to be prophets who, by reminding, point their people in a new direction and guide them into unknown territory. Therefore, I would like to speak now about the minister as a guiding reminder. Again, three areas call for our attention: the guidance, the guiding and the guide.

THE GUIDANCE

Good memories offer good guidance. We all have had the experience that in times of distress, failure and depression it is the good memories which give us new confidence and hope. When the night is dark and everything seems black and fearful, we can hope for a bright new day because we have seen a bright day before. Our hope is built on our memories. Without memories there are no expectations. We do not always realize that among the best things we can give each other are good memories: kind words, signs of affection, gestures of sympathy, peaceful silences and joyful celebrations. At the time they all may have seemed obvious, simple, and without many consequences, but as memories they can save us in the midst of confusion, fear and darkness.

When we speak about guiding memories we do not necessarily refer to a conscious remembering, an explicit reflection on events in the past. In fact, most of our memories guide us in a prereflective way. They have become flesh and blood in us. Our memories of trust, love, acceptance, forgiveness, confidence and

266

hope enter so deeply into our being that indeed we become our memories. The fact that we are alive, that our hearts beat, our blood flows, our lungs breathe, is a living memory of all the good care that came our way. It is primarily such incarnate, pulsating memories that carry us through our dark moments and give us hope. These memories might be dormant during our normal day-to-day living, but in times of crisis they often reveal their great revitalizing power.

It is to these conscious and unconscious memories that the great prophets in history have appealed. The prophets of Israel guided their people first of all by reminding them. Hear how Moses guides his people: 'Remember how Yahweh led you out of Egypt ... follow his ways and pay reverence to him' (cf. Deuteronomy 8:2–14). 'Do not mistreat strangers, remember that once you were a stranger' (cf. Exodus 22:20; Deuteronomy 10:19). Listen to the indignant Isaiah: 'Stir your memories again, you sinners, remember things long past. I am God unrivalled, God who has no like. From the beginning I foretold the future, and predicted beforehand what is to be' (Isa. 46:8–10).

By reminding their people of the misery of slavery and the liberating love of God, the prophets of Israel motivated them to move forward, and challenged them to honour their memory by their behaviour. As living reminders of God's care and compassion, they unmasked the stifling and narrow-minded viewpoints of their contemporaries and again disclosed the vision that inspired their forefathers and that still offers constant guidance in the continuing search for salvation.

In Jesus this prophetic ministry finds its fullest expression. In His teaching he reminds His contemporaries of their own history, confronts them with their limited views, and challenges them to recognize God's guiding presence in their lives. He evokes the memory of Elijah and Elisha, Jonah and Solomon. He tries to break through the fearful resistance of His followers and open their hearts to the unlimited love of His Father. Everything Jesus tells His disciples about the need for repentance and the love of the Father He tells them so that they will remember during the difficult times ahead. 'I have told you all this so that when the time comes, you will remember' (John 16:4).

And so they did. As Jesus reminded His disciples of the Father, so the disciples remind each other and their followers of Jesus. In memory of Jesus they speak, preach, witness, and break bread; in memory of Jesus they find the strength to live through tribulations and persecutions. In short, it is the memory of Jesus that guides them and offers them hope and confidence in the midst of a failing culture, a faltering society, and a dark world.

So our memories give us guidance. They are the blueprint for our future. They help us to move forward faithful to the vision which made us leave the land of slavery, and obedient to the call which says that the promised land is still ahead of us.

THE GUIDING

How do ministers, as living memories of Jesus Christ, guide their people in the concrete circumstances of everyday life? Two ways of guiding suggest themselves in the context of this discussion on memory: confronting and inspiring. It may be surprising to think of confrontation as a form of guidance, but a prophetic ministry which guides towards a new future requires the hard, painful unmasking of our illusions: the illusion that 'we have arrived', that we have found the final articulation of our faith, and that we have discovered the life-style which best gives shape to our ideals. We are constantly tempted to replace the original vision with a rather comfortable interpretation of that vision. It is this complacent and stifling narrowing down of the vision to our own needs and aspirations that all reformers have confronted with their prophetic ministries. Benedict in the sixth century, Francis in the twelfth, Martin Luther in the sixteenth, John Wesley in the eighteenth, and people such as Dorothy Day and Mother Teresa today – all of them have confronted the ways in which the great vision has become blurred and has lost its convincing appeal. Guidance requires the breaking down of these false walls and the removal of obstacles to growth. People caught in mental and spiritual chains cannot be guided.

But guidance demands more than confrontation. It requires recapturing the original vision, going back to the point from which the great inspiration came. In this sense all reformers are revisionists, people who remind us of the great vision. Benedict recaptured the vision of community, Francis recaptured the vision of poverty, Luther recaptured the vision of God's undeserved grace, Wesley recaptured the vision of a living faith, and today many prophets are recapturing the vision of peace and justice. They all have moved backwards, not in sentimental melancholy but in the conviction that from a recaptured vision new life can develop. The French have an imaginative expression: *recular pour mieux sauter*, to step back in order to jump farther. Ministers who guide step back in order to touch again the best memories of their community and so to remind their people of the original vision. The paradox of progress is that it occurs by conserving the great memory which can revitalize dormant dreams.

Thus the minister guides by confronting and inspiring. Confrontation challenges us to confess and repent; inspiration stirs us to look up again with new courage and confidence.

How might such confrontation and inspiration express themselves in our daily ministry? I will limit myself to only one concrete suggestion: tell a story. Often colourful people of great faith will confront and inspire more readily than the pale doctrines of faith. The Epistle to the Hebrews does not offer

269

general ideas about how to move forward but calls to mind the great people in history: Abel, Enoch, Noah, Abraham, Sarah, Isaac, Jacob, Moses, and many others. And then it says, 'With so many witnesses in a great cloud on every side of us, we too, then, should throw off everything that hinders us, especially the sin that clings so easily, and keep running steadily in the race we have started' (Hebrews 12:1).

We guide by calling to mind men and women in whom the great vision becomes visible, people with whom we can identify, yet people who have broken out of the constraints of their time and place and moved into unknown fields with great courage and confidence. The rabbis guide their people with stories; ministers usually guide with ideas and theories. We need to become storytellers again, and so multiply our ministry by calling around us the great witnesses who in different ways offer guidance to doubting hearts.

One of the remarkable qualities of the story is that it creates space. We can dwell in a story, walk around, find our own place. The story confronts but does not oppress; the story inspires but does not manipulate. The story invites us to an encounter, a dialogue, a mutual sharing.

A story that guides is a story that opens a door and offers us space in which to search and boundaries to help us find what we seek, but it does not tell us what to do or how to do it. The story brings us into touch with the vision and so guides us. Wiesel writes, 'God made man because he loves stories.'[4] As long as we have stories to tell to each other there is hope. As long as we can remind each other of the lives of men and women in whom the love of God becomes manifest, there is reason to move forward to new land in which new stories are hidden.

[4] Wiesel, *The Gates of the Forest*, flyleaf.

THE GUIDE

What are the implications of this understanding of guidance for the spiritual life of ministers? They are many, and they all cut deeply into our way of being attentive to the world. But they all point to the need to be in touch with the source from which the guiding inspiration comes. It is clear from what we have already said that we cannot guide others by a simple argument, some casual advice, a few instructions, or an occasional sermon. Prophecy confronts and inspires only insofar as prophets are indeed speaking from the vision which guides their own lives day and night. It is in the encounter with the prophetic minister that strength is found to break out of myopic viewpoints and courage is given to move beyond safe and secure boundaries.

I have asked many people for counsel in my own personal and professional life. The more I reflect on this, the more I realize that I experience guidance and hope, not because of any specific suggestion or advice but because of a strength far beyond their own awareness which radiated from my counsellors. On the other hand, I have tried to help many people and have been increasingly surprised that I often gave strength when I least expected to and received grateful notes when I thought that I had been of no help at all. It seems that we often reveal and communicate to others the life-giving spirit without being aware of it. One of the most comforting remarks I ever heard was: 'I wish you could experience yourself as I experience you. Then you would not be so depressed.' The great mystery of ministry is that while we ourselves are overwhelmed by our own weaknesses and limitations, we can still be so transparent that the Spirit of God, the divine counsellor, can shine through us and bring light to others.

How then can we be spiritual people through whom God's divine counsellor and guide can become manifest? If we really

271

want to be living memories, offering guidance to a new land, the word of God must be engraved in our hearts; it must become our flesh and blood. That means much more than intellectual reflection. It means meditating and ruminating on God's word – chewing it or, as the Psalmist puts it, 'murmuring' it day and night. In this way the word of God can slowly descend from our mind into our heart and so fill us with the life-giving Spirit. This 'total' meditation on the Word of God lies deeply embedded in the rabbinic as well as the Christian tradition. Jean Leclercq, the Benedictine medieval scholar, writes:

> ... to meditate is to read a text and to learn it 'by heart' in the fullest sense of this expression, that is, with one's whole being: with the body since the mouth pronounced it, with the memory which fixes it, with the intelligence which under-stands its meaning and with the will which desires to put it in practice.[5]

This meditation on God's Word is indispensable if we want to be reminders of God and not of ourselves, if we want to radiate hope and not despair, joy and not sadness, life and not death. Since the greatest news is that the Word has become flesh, it is indeed our greatest vocation and obligation to continue this divine incarnation through daily meditation on the Word.

While any specific prayer technique is secondary to our obli-gation to meditate, and although every individual has to find his own way, a disregard for techniques in prayer is just as unwise as a disregard for techniques and skill in pastoral care. The his-tory of Jewish and Christian spirituality shows that our most precious relationship, our relationship with God, cannot simply

---

[5] Jean Leclercq, *The Love of Learning and the Desire for God: A Study of Monastic Culture* (New York: Fordham University Press, 1961), pp. 21, 22.

be left to our spontaneous outpourings. Precisely because God is central to our lives, our relationship with Him calls for formation and training, including skills and methods. Therefore, it is sad that most ministers have more hours of training in how to talk and be with people than how to talk and be with God. There are even seminaries which feel that the question of how to pray is not a question to which the faculty can respond. Yet how can we guide people with God's Word if that word is more a subject for discussion and debate than for meditation? It is not the disembodied word that guides, but the word that pervades our whole earthly being and manifests itself in all we do and say.

One simple and somewhat obvious technique is memorization. The expression 'to know by heart' already suggests its value. Personally I regret the fact that I know so few prayers and psalms by heart. Often I need a book to pray, and without one I tend to fall back on the poor spontaneous creations of my mind. Part of the reason, I think, that it is so hard to pray 'without ceasing' is that few prayers are available to me outside church settings. Yet I believe that prayers which I know by heart could carry me through very painful crises. The Methodist minister Fred Morris told me how Psalm 23 ('The Lord is my shepherd') had carried him through the gruesome hours in the Brazilian torture chamber and had given him peace in his darkest hour. And I keep wondering which words I can take with me in the hour when I have to survive without books. I fear that in crisis situations I will have to depend on my own unredeemed ramblings and not have the word of God to guide me.

Perhaps the 1970s offer us a unique chance to reclaim the rich tradition of schooling in prayer. All spiritual writers, from the desert fathers to Teresa of Avila, Evelyn Underhill and Thomas Merton, have stressed the great power and central importance of prayer in our lives. Theophan the Recluse expresses this forcefully when he says:

> Prayer is the test of everything; prayer is also the source of everything; prayer is the driving force of everything; prayer is also the director of everything. If prayer is right, everything is right. For prayer will not allow anything to go wrong.[6]

If this is true, then it is obvious that prayer requires supervision and direction. Just as verbatim reports of our conversations with patients can help us to deepen our interpersonal sensitivities, so a continuing evaluation of our spiritual life can lead us closer to God. If we do not hesitate to study how love and care reveal themselves in encounters between people, then why should we shy away from detailed attention to the relationship with Him who is the source and purpose of all human interactions? The fact that many of the spiritual movements of our day seem to be irresponsible, manipulative, and even downright dangerous for the mental and physical health of the people involved, makes it urgent that the spiritual life of ministers and future ministers not be left to their own uninformed experimentations.

There is little doubt that seminaries and centres for Clinical Pastoral Education are challenged to incorporate the spiritual formation of the students into their programmes. This will be far from easy and there are many pitfalls, but denying the increasing spiritual needs of students and ministers will only backfire in the form of a growing amateurism in this most sensitive area of contemporary experience.

Many ministers today are excellent preachers, competent counsellors, and good programme administrators, but few feel comfortable giving spiritual direction to people who are searching for God's presence in their lives. For many ministers, if not for most, the life of the Holy Spirit is unknown territory. It is not surprising, therefore, that many unholy spirits have taken over

---

[6] *The Art of Prayer*, p. 51.

and created considerable havoc. There is an increasing need for diagnosticians of the soul who can distinguish the Holy Spirit from the unholy spirits and so guide people to an active and vital transformation of soul and body, and of all their personal relationships.[7] This gift of discernment is a gift of the Spirit which can only be received through constant prayer and meditation.

Thus the spiritual life of the minister, formed and trained in a school of prayer, is the core of spiritual leadership. When we have lost the vision, we have nothing to show; when we have forgotten the Word of God, we have nothing to remember; when we have buried the blueprint of our life, we have nothing to build. But when we keep in touch with the life-giving spirit within us, we can lead people out of their captivity and become hope-giving guides.

CONCLUSION

I have tried to make three points in this discussion of the minister as a guiding reminder. First, our hope in the future is built on our conscious and unconscious memories. Second, guiding takes place by unmasking the illusion of present comfort and reminding people of the original vision. Third, this vision becomes flesh and blood by an unceasing meditation on the Word of God.

All this means that to be guiding ministers, we must be prophets who, by appealing to memories, encourage our fellow human beings to move forward. Let me summarize what this says about our lives as ministers.

[7] Ibid., p. 119.

It says that we need to think about ways to make our individual and collective memories a source of guidance.

It says that we should look at guidance as a form of prophecy.

It says that we should rediscover the art of story-telling as a ministerial art.

It says that meditation is indispensible for a real incarnation of the Word of God in our lives.

Finally, it says that we need to explore ways to introduce schooling in prayer into pastoral education.

Epilogue
A Professing Profession

When I finished writing these chapters about the minister as a living reminder of Jesus Christ, I realized that, in fact, I had discussed the minister as pastor, as priest, and as prophet. As pastors, ministers heal the wounds of the past; as priests, they sustain life in the present; and as prophets, they guide others to the future. They do all of this in memory of Him who is, who was, and is to come. When I became aware of how traditional I had been, I felt a little embarrassed at first. But then I realized that, after all, my only real task had been to be a reminder of what we already know.

What I have tried to do is to look at the biblical roles of ministry in the context of the new developments in pastoral psychology and thus to unite two aspects of the ministry as a profession. Profession as we conceive of it today primarily suggests training, skill, expertise, and a certain specialization. Theological education in recent decades has made a major contribution towards establishing the ministry as a profession in a highly professionalized world. But 'profession' also refers to professing, witnessing, proclaiming, announcing. This professing side of our ministerial life, which is deeply rooted in our biblical heritage, requires formation as well. Profession as expertise and profession as proclamation can never be separated without harm. When we profess our faith in Christ without any ministerial expertise, we are like people shouting from the mountain top without caring if anyone is listening. But when we are skilful experts who have little to profess, then we easily become lukewarm technicians who squeeze God's work between 9 a.m. and 5 p.m.

One of our most challenging tasks today is to explore our spiritual resources and to integrate the best of what we find there with the best of what we have found in the behavioural sciences. When psychiatrists, psychologists, medical doctors, and other professionals ask us, 'Tell me, how are you different from us?' we must be able to hear that question as a challenge to transcend the boundaries of our technocratic society and to proclaim with renewed fervour that the Lord is risen, is risen indeed. The temptation remains to forget our proclaiming task and to settle for an easy professionalism. But I am convinced that deep in our heart there is voice that keeps calling us back to the hard but joyful task of proclaiming the good news.

Let me conclude with the story of the disenchanted rabbi who:

> was weary of threatening sinners with the wrath of Yahweh … and of comforting the meek with his goodness. And so, deserting his synagogue, he set off on his wanderings in disguise. He came to an old woman who lay dying in her drafty hovel. 'Why was I born,' asked the old woman, 'when as long as I can remember nothing but misfortune has been my lot?' 'That you should bear it,' was the disguised rabbi's reply, and it set the dying woman's mind at rest. As he drew the sheet over her face, he decided that from then on he would be mute. On the third day of his wanderings, he encountered a young beggar girl, carrying her dead child on her back. The rabbi helped to dig the grave; shrouding the tiny corpse in linen, they laid it in the pit, covered it up, broke bread, and to the

beggar girl's every word the rabbi answered with gestures. 'The poor thing got nothing, neither pleasure nor pain. Do you think it was worth his being born?' At first the rabbi in disguise made no move, but when the girl insisted, he nodded. Thereupon he decided to be deaf as well as dumb. He hid away from the world in a cave. There he met no one, only a ferret. Its foot was hurt, so the rabbi bound it with herbs; whereupon the tiny ferret brought his tasty seeds. The hermit prayed, the tiny beast wiggled its nose, and the two grew fond of one another. One afternoon a condor plummeted from a great height, and as the ferret was basking in the sun at the mouth of the cave, carried it off before the rabbi's eyes. At that, the rabbi thought to himself that it would be better if he closed his eyes too. But since – blind, dumb, and deaf – he could do nothing but wait for death, which, he felt, it was not seemly to hasten, he girded his loins and returned to his congregation. Once again he preached to them on the subject of good and evil, according to Yahweh's law. He did what he had done before and waxed strong in his shame.[1]

We often may want to run away from our home to hide out and play deaf, dumb, and blind for a while. But we are ministers. Not only dying and lonely people but even little ferrets remind us of that. And so we keep returning to our people, faithful to our vocation, and growing strong in humility and love.

[1] George Konrad, *The Case Worker* (New York: Harcourt Brace Jovanovich, 1974), pp.130–131.